EATING
AGAIN

EATING AGAIN

THE RECIPES THAT HEALED ME

ALICE CARBONE TENCH

 Heliotrope Books

NEW YORK

ISBN 978-1-942762-78-2
ISBN 978-1-942762-80-5 eBook

Food photography: *Alice Carbone Tench*

Cover photo: *Roman Cho*

Cover design: *Naomi Rosenblatt*

The following recipes were photographed by *Andrew MacPherson*:
Stuffed Tomatoes, Peperonata, Bread Meatballs, Bicerin of Turin, and Chocolate "Salami"

Food Styling: *Alice Carbone Tench* and *Erica Canales*

Production and lighting: *Erica Canales*

Hair and Makeup: *Erica Canales*

To Catherine

May this book be for you a window into your roots,
to always remember where you come from.
May these recipes remind you of me when I'll be gone
and may Italian food guide you when
you'll be hungry for more,
for change, for life.

And to Cei and Diane

I wouldn't have sliced the first onion
if it hadn't been for you.
I love you very much.

CONTENTS

ICONIC RECIPES FROM INSTAGRAM •101

SOUPS, SAUCES, DIPS, AND STEWS THAT TASTE LIKE HOME •163

WHAT DOES HOME TASTE LIKE? •165

PREGNANCY AND EATING DISORDERS •188

RECIPES INSPIRED BY MY MOM •193

THANK YOU, TOM •219

CAKES, TARTS, AND PUDDINGS •223

ACKNOWLEDGMENTS •249
APPENDIX A: FOOD SUBSTITUTIONS •250
APPENDIX B: PREPARING AND FREEZING •252
APPENDIX C: A NOTE ON TOMATO SAUCE •253

INTRODUCTION

never meant to write a cookbook. When I began to cook on Instagram, in the spring of 2018, I did it because I needed help; I needed to be seen and heard. I think I needed witnesses, in my audience, to hold me accountable in my personal recovery from eating disorders. I also needed support in my healing journey as a new mother and wife who had lost herself as a woman.

My two wonderful therapists, Cei and Diane, had suggested food as a means of getting back in touch with myself a long time before the first recipe went on camera. But I wasn't ready when they first had suggested that I mindfully slice an onion, staying in whatever discomfort, or ease, I'd discover. I didn't know that I was a good cook, I didn't know that I could remember all the recipes from my childhood, and I didn't know how much I loved cooking.

No, I never meant to write a cookbook, but I need my recipes written somewhere so that Catherine can find them when she grows up, and so I won't have to log onto my website every time I forget an ingredient.

That's how I began to write this book.

As I went through each recipe, I would find similarities and connections between the essays I was writing on my blog and the stories behind every dish.

And so, this book wrote itself.

A few years ago, I had tried to write a food memoir tentatively titled *The Year I Began to Cook*, but nothing was right about it—the agent, the stories, and the way every feeling felt forced, wrong, uncomfortable.

Nothing about this book was ever forced, difficult, or unpleasant. It's the first time in my life that I have experienced a level of easiness, trust, and comfort that words can hardly describe.

This book was meant to be.

With every dish and every story, I want to share with you the ingredients of my favorite recipe: the one that made me the woman I am today, a woman I often struggle with, and yet a woman I finally love and respect. These are the recipes that healed me.

I want to give you access to the story of a curious 8-year-old in the Italian Alps approaching the kitchen for the first time, and also of a young woman suffering from bulimia who ran away from it, and ultimately of a mother and a wife who traveled across the world to rediscover her roots and the ingredients to a life worth loving.

Most of the food I make, as you know or will soon discover, is very open to personalization; the quantities are rarely set in stone. I love dishes that can be adapted, and that allow cooks and food lovers to explore their creativity, discover new flavors, new directions, new combinations, and new ingredients. I am not a trained chef. I didn't go to culinary school. I learned to cook by watching my mother and my grandmother, and it is from them that I learned the art of tasting, of observing, and of trusting my hands and my instinct with salt, sugar, oil, or herbs.

As my recovery progressed, I began to be more and more involved in the social aspect of food. Part of my work in the field is doing everything I can to create a society in which culinary self-care (which means culinary joy, health, positivity, and bounty), is not a luxury. Healthy food, the pleasure of food, and the knowledge we access in order to make good choices when we buy groceries shouldn't be prohibitive, unsustainable, or something for only the richest.

Ben's life motto is "live a good life and help others do the same." As my blessings in life grew, so did my eagerness to make sure I did just that. I happen to do it from the kitchen.

So, please have fun with these recipes! Use each as a canvas, and paint your version of it. Keep an open mind, don't be afraid, and never merely endure food. Never merely endure life. This life, like a good pantry, has all the tools and the ingredients for the best possible meal!

Set the table, and *buon appetito!*

NOTE

For precision, all the recipes are in metric system (grams, milliliters, etc.). That's how I have created them, with my Italian brain, but I have also added a conversion for your convenience.

However, if you can—and especially for baking—invest in a small kitchen scale that will always give you the most accurate measurement for guaranteed success.

Some followers from Instagram to Table could not find various ingredients that I work with and asked about substitutes. You will find a list of those recommendations in Appendix A of this book. In Appendices B and C I include tips for handling and freezing other ingredients. I would love to know how these tips work out for you; I am always more than happy to discuss them on my socials, or through my website. Cooking has been, for me at least, a social activity. So, everything is an act of sharing and learning from each other.

MY GRANDMOTHER'S DIARIES
from 2015

When my grandmother died on July 30th of 2001, she left me all her diaries—30 years of life from when I hadn't yet been born to the day of her death, when my grandfather wrote *fine* (the end) on the last page.

A few years ago, during a trip to Italy, Ben and I flew with extra empty suitcases in which to bring all the diaries back home to Los Angeles. "Do you think I'm invading her privacy?" I had asked my mom before opening the first one.

Did I have the right to read what she confided to the page in secret? As a writer myself, I had to ask such a question: Where is the line between private and public, when it comes to writing?

"Why don't you ask her?" my mother suggested. "Ask what she thinks. Stay still, in silence, and you will hear the answer. She will speak to you."

I did. I sat down quietly before opening the first diary, I closed my eyes and I asked her: "Give me a sign, Madri" (the affectionate name I used to call her). "Can I read your diaries? Am I doing the right thing?"

There isn't a day when I don't feel her presence in my life, her protection, her comfort, and her guidance. One of her diaries is always on my desk, the one from 2001. From the desk she also looks at me through the film of a photograph; she looks melancholic but smiles genuinely, elegant, with perfectly sculpted thin eyebrows and no makeup other than red lipstick. She looks exactly as I remember her, loving and yet austere.

Madri is always with me. Wherever I go, I bring with me the rosary she brought me from one of her yearly trips to Lourdes, one that becomes fluorescent in the dark.

When my grandfather became very ill with a life-threatening stomach infection and fought for his life, I believe in the early 1980s, my grandmother had prayed to the Virgin Mary of Lourdes and promised she would go to Lourdes every year in a sign of gratitude if my grandfather survived. He did survive, Grandpa Arrigo, and she kept the promise. With my grandfather, she went to Lourdes every year until 2001, when she passed away.

I don't keep the rosary in my purse for religious reasons; I keep the rosary because it reminds me of times when everything felt okay, when I felt safe.

So that day, when I asked: "Can I read your diaries? Am I doing the right thing?" She made sure I could hear her answer: All of a sudden, I experienced a renewed sense of serenity, her warm embrace, something in the air and throughout my body that made me feel okay. It wasn't happiness; it wasn't joy, but a sense that everything was taken care of, and that I was on the right path.

I read every story, every good day and every bad day, weeks of sun and weeks of rain, from the mountains or from the beach. I read every menu, every bill that my grandfather and she paid, every joy, and every frustration.

The sense of discomfort that I'd sometimes experience when coming across episodes of my childhood that I only vaguely remembered, or sometimes wasn't aware of at all, soon became acceptance, understanding, and compassion. Some details I could have guessed, others left me helpless, full of regrets, and very sad. I hadn't understood how much my grandmother loved me, but I knew how much we shared, how much we both suffered, and how much the act of writing about it gave us some relief.

I didn't start writing until much later in life, but I remember trying for years to keep a diary like she did. No matter how tired she was, every night before going to bed, she would write a few words about the day that had just ended. I never had that rigor, that discipline. So, I look at her stories, written with simple words and a mix of Italian and Piedmont dialect (*Piemontese*), and feel a lot of respect for her, for how she made of a simple and humble life, not an easy one, something always worth noting on paper. I think I learned from her that every story is worth sharing.

But there was one more link between the two of us: Food.

Even when stories were permeated by sadness, by difficulties and hardships, she always wrote what she ate, what she cooked, the menus at events that she and my grandfather attended, and the food she ate in the hospital during the several times she was hospitalized for depression.

"Ben, read this," I'd call to him at almost every page. "I so remember when she'd make kale and potato soup, or tuna with eggs and tomato sauce...I loved it."

I remembered much more than I initially thought—like going mushroom picking with her and my grandfather, reciting the rosary in the sanctuary by the lake throughout the month of May. I remembered daily slivers of life together, such as walking from my elementary school to their place every day for lunch.

It wasn't a long walk, 5 minutes at the most, and not really a beautiful one, but I remember it as peaceful, without too much traffic, mostly for pedestrians; I remember passing the playground where younger kids, not yet of age for school, played, and the side of the street where plenty of stinging nettles grew, those same stinging nettles my grandmother would transform into a risotto (recipe follows), a soup, a frittata.

Playing in their garage with my brother was also very clear in my memory; we usually played there when my grandfather was fixing shoes in the back, and we had fun gardening, planting tomatoes and kale, and then drinking fresh water from a metal cup that seemed to have been there forever, by the sink, just next to the wine barrel.

I remember taking a bath at their house every Tuesday night, when we'd sleep over. Their bathroom, with a dark orange carpet, was very small, and it always smelled like my grandfather's shower gel—like a pine tree, in fact called Pino Silvestre. The tub was so short that we couldn't completely lie down; it was more of a "sitting-bath" situation. Even though the room was somber, I felt the view from the window, looking over the other small orchard they had, made the bathroom look royal.

I smiled every time I read about the long afternoons playing in our bedroom, which used to be my great grandmother's, and in which Madri kept most of her accessories—her hats, sewing kit, and knitting tools.

I used to wear her clothes, her jewelry, and the wig she would wear when she wanted to look different for a night out with my grandfather. I'd pretend to be an old lady, with Madri's hair that always seemed to have some glittery hair spray on it.

This is what food does to me: It takes me places, it takes me back, it awakens memories, and it heals the sense of loss, of regret, and of fear. Food brings me closer to Madri, to my past, and to what I strive every day to preserve and share with my family and friends.

It was my grandmother's cooking that influenced me the most; everything she cooked was a feast, for me. Lunch at her house, every day after school, was the most beautiful time of day. The tiny kitchenette with its turquoise table and cabinets became my culinary Disneyland.

"What's for lunch, Madri?" I'd ask, always hungry.

"Hearts and lungs," she would say one day. I'd smile, helping my grandfather set the table, and counting down the seconds to finally eat one of my favorite delicacies. The kitchen was so small that after I sat, with my back against a long cabinet, they pushed the table toward me so that three or four people would fit—usually my grandparents, my brother, and me.

My grandfather always sat at the end of the table against the fridge. He was in charge of the wine, which he made in the garage across the street, and of grating Parmesan cheese for everyone. Madri sat at the other end, with her back to the window, and with easy access to the stove and the sink. I can still see her, standing by the stove, turning off the heat, and walking to the table where my grandfather and I waited. I loved my grandparents.

The stew of beef hearts and lungs, with onion and red wine, was one of her specialties. She served it regularly and I couldn't get enough. My mother hated onions, so she would never cook them at home. I loved onions, and my grandmother would always find endless ways to serve them, whether stuffed with meat, in the stew, in a frittata, or in her signature tomato sauce. The sweetness and the embracing, gentle flavor of onions is one taste that I recall most vividly, and that brings me back to that house, to those years, to the past.

If I close my eyes today, I can still taste the onion melting in my mouth, cooked for hours in the stew, and then the crunchiness of the hearts against the irresistible sponginess of the lungs. I loved her stuffed bell peppers, her stuffed onions, and her stuffed zucchini, that she made with meat, cabbage, eggs, and lots of parmesan cheese.

Every Wednesday we would have *granelle* (Rocky Mountain oysters), and the rest of the week was always a surprise. Maybe we would have breaded veal brain sautéed with butter, ground raw meat salad with carrot salad, tongue with green parsley sauce, kidney stew, chicken liver with onions, Milanese, *spezzatino* (beef stew) with wild mushrooms, wild herbs frittata, wild herbs soup, milk and rice soup, breaded trout, handmade gnocchi with tomato sauce, and agnolotti stuffed with her secret recipe of veal, pork, and cabbage.

Every time we had rabbit, another traditional dish where I am from, my grandfather and I would share the head; I can still taste the crunchy little tongue, and soft, creamy brain. My favorite part was the meat around the chest, so that I could clean (eating) every little bone.

I don't eat meat anymore, and when I think about these dishes so dear to my heart, I can't help but meditate on the passing of time, on change, on how we all want and need it, and yet struggle to entirely accept it when faced with it.

For a long time, I thought I missed meat for its taste, but as I continued to think about the real object of my longing, my certainty began to fade.

When I was growing up, in the mid-1980s, there was no internet, no social media, no access to research, not really an awareness about climate change and animal suffering.

Did I miss meat, or did I miss the past? Did I miss the food, or did I miss childhood?

The longer I wrote about the food, the clearer the answer became: What I missed was not the culinary experience, but rather the time in my life when I was still shielded from decisions and responsibilities, from having to choose for the greater good.

After lunch, Madri would wash the dishes, looking out the window where my grandfather's orchard was, rich in spinach, kale, collard greens, and several varieties of lettuce. My grandfather made the coffee and cleared the table; he would always shake the tablecloth outside, so that birds could have their lunch, too.

"Can you wash this, please?" I'd ask, handing her the jaw of the rabbit, where the two front teeth were still attached. She would clean it, then hand it to me dry, and I'd play with it as she and my grandfather drank their coffee, in a drinking glass, with sugar but no milk.

I'd sit with them playing with my new toy, and I waited for the bottom of their coffee, where some of the sugar had not completely melted, and that I would eat with a spoon.

I never had a sweet tooth, but that coffee-flavored sugar was my treat after the meal.

I won't be able to cook for Catherine every recipe that my grandmother made for me, but thanks to her writing, I'll be able to share the stories, the ingredients, her passion for food, and how special that time was.

MENU

Gennaio 15 - Pranzo gruppo funghi - £15000 / salame - pasta asciutta - arrosto di tacchino patate - frutta - dolce - caffè

29 - Pranzo cooperatori / affettati - tomini - risotto al merluzzo arrosto - patate - dolce - formaggio - frutta £ 25000

Febbraio 5 Pranzo Murzu e Moteano - Gamberetti salmone - bresaola tomini - vitello tonnato - risotto composrolo - cappelletti in brodo - filetto e patate al forno - polenta e fonduè dolce - macedonia e gelato - caffè £ 40000

12 Pranzo del comune per auxiani al Mega - prosciutto crudo con Kiwi - affettati misti - vitello tonnato - tolton con funghi - frittata di prosciutto - agnolotti - tagliatelle - tortellini in brodo - arrosto - pollo - patate - spinaci - insalata e dolci - frutta - caffè £ 25000

Marzo 25 prosciutto con ananas - vitello tonnato - gamberetti in salsa boccancini di trota in cartoccio - crêpe crema di funghi cotechino con patate duchessa - pere alla mus di formaggio crespelle alla valdostana - lasagne verdi al forno - cappelletti in brodo - porchetta alla romana - bocconcini al curry patatine - spinaci e carote - dolce della casa - gelato - caffè

Settembre 7 ex allieve - affettati - 2 qualità di agnolotti mus di mare £ 55000 arrosto - patate fritte insalata formaggio - dolce gelato caffè offerto tecole £ 50000 di offerta

Ottobre 7 - chiusura salesiani - aperitivo - affettati - bue affumicato - robiola con tartufo - salamini con purè - carne all'ese capricciosa - risotto con funghi - agnolotti al ragù sorbetto - fritto misto - cosciotto al forno con purè polenta con cinghiale ai funghi - torta - macedonia con gelato - caffè - puro caffè £ 60000

Novembre 5 Pranzo e castagnate S. Maria - manzo affumicato - lingua al verde - vitello tonnato - sfogliatine ai funghi - tartrè con salsiccia al barolo - peperoni con bagno cauda gnocchi alla bava - nidi di rondine ai funghi -

An excerpt (translated) *from a menu I have found in my grandmother's diary from 1995:*

January, Lunch with the Family Group, 25.000 Lire:
Cold-cuts plate, tomino cheese, cod risotto, roast meat, oven-roasted potatoes, dessert, assorted cheese, fruit

February, Lunch with the Elders Group 20.000 Lire:
Prosciutto with kiwi, cold-cuts plate, veal with tuna and caper sauce (vitello tonnato), vol-au-vent with mushroom, frittata with prosciutto, agnolotti pasta, tagliatelle, and small ravioli (tortelli) with vegetable broth, roast meat, chicken and potatoes, spinach, salad, two desserts, fruit, coffee.

September, school reunion, 50.000 Lire:
Cold-cuts plate, seafood salad, agnolotti pasta two ways, roast, fried potatoes, salad, assorted cheese, ice cream, hazelnut biscotti, coffee

October, lunch with the Salesians of Don Bosco, 60.000 Lire:
Aperitif with cold-cuts plate, smoked ox, truffle robiola cheese, chopped raw beef (carne albese), Capricciosa salad (Italian coleslaw), porcini mushroom risotto, agnolotti pasta with ragù sauce, sorbet, mixed fry, chicken tight with mashed potatoes, polenta with wild boar and mushrooms, cake, fruit salad with ice cream, coffee, digestive liquor (*pusa café, which in the local dialect literally means a drink that pushed the coffee down*)

November, S. Cecilia with D. Roberto 20.000 Lire:
Chopped raw meat (carne all'albese), scampi with cocktail sauce, bagna cauda with mixed vegetables, agnolotti pasta with tomato sauce, risotto with aromatic herbs, roast meat with sautéed carrots and spinach, fruit salad, assorted dessert made by the women in the choir.

December, Dinner Brodolini, 67.000 Lire:
Vol-au-vent with fondue, ham rolls with asparagus, salami and lentils, salmon crostini, carne albese, capricciosa, sorbet, mushroom tagliolini pasta, agnolotti with tomato sauce, crepes with porcini mushroom, roast meat with chanterelle mushrooms, polenta with wild boar, robiola cheese, chocolate and hazelnut cake, panna cotta, tiramisu, profiteroles, spumante, coffee, and digestive.

RECIPES INSPIRED BY MY GRANDMOTHER

MADRI'S ONION FRITTATA

FOR 6 PEOPLE

Onion frittata is a simple dish that, more than anything else reminds me of my grandmother's food. Onions, in fact, were forbidden in my house. My mom hated both the smell and the flavor, so she never cooked them, never added them to sauces or sautés, never even bought them. I love onions. And this frittata is straightforward: onions, eggs, and parmesan cheese. My grandmother used to make it all the time, and I can still remember the sweetness of the onions, their warm aroma when sautéed in a good extra-virgin olive oil. The section of this book dedicated to her had to start with this.

Preparation: 10 minutes
Cooking time: 15 minutes

7 eggs
3 medium onions or 2 big ones
¼ cup parmesan cheese
1 one small sprig of thyme (or sage and rosemary)
Salt, pepper, and olive oil to taste

Peel the onions and slice them finely with a mandolin.

Sauté the onions in extra-virgin olive oil until well caramelized (the caramelization is what gives the onion a magical flavor). I like to infuse the onions with fresh herbs such as sage, thyme, and rosemary. Remove the herbs after the onions are ready, before adding them to the egg mixture.

In a mixing bowl, beat the eggs with salt, black pepper, and thyme; if you want, here, you can add some bread previously softened in a glass of milk. Squeeze the milk out and add to the egg mixture.

Add the caramelized onions to the egg mixture.

Pour into a non-stick skillet with some olive oil, lower the heat to low-medium and cover. Cook, untouched, for a good 10 minutes (I like to cook one side very well, because it makes it easier to flip the frittata).

After 10 minutes, check on the frittata. If the eggs start to be cooked on top and they are well cooked along the edges, it's the perfect time to flip the frittata onto the lid and then slide it gently back into the skillet, to cook the other side for 5 minutes. The trick to a perfect flipping is the cooking point of the top of the frittata.

Let it rest for 5 minutes and then enjoy. This frittata is beautiful the day after, especially in a panino, or simply with a radicchio salad. Its bitterness goes beautifully with the buttery sweetness of the onions.

KALE AND CHERRY TOMATO FRITTATA

FOR 6 PEOPLE

Frittatas are one of my favorite ways to clean the fridge, but also to mix vegetables for Catherine. The combination of kale and tomatoes, in this case, turned to be one of our favorites during the summer season, when cherry tomatoes are at their best. You can substitute the kale with spinach, chard, even collard greens.

Preparation: 10 minutes
Cooking time: 15 minutes

7 eggs
4-5 leaves of kale
¼ cup parmesan cheese (or to taste)
2 leeks or 3 spring onions
½ cup cherry tomatoes
Salt, pepper, and olive oil to taste
3-4 leaves of fresh basil

Rinse the kale and chop it finely.

Rinse the leeks or the spring onions, remove the tops and the first three layers, then thinly slice them with a mandolin.

Sauté the leeks and kale in extra-virgin olive oil until cooked through, then set aside and allow to cool down for a few minutes.

In a mixing bowl, beat the eggs with salt and black pepper; slice the cherry tomatoes in half, and add them to the egg mixture, as well as the chopped basil and the grated cheese.

Add the sautéed kale and leeks.

Pour into a non-stick skillet with some olive oil, lower the heat to low-medium, and cover with a lid.

Cook, untouched, for a good 5 minutes (I like to cook one side very well, because it makes it easier to flip the frittata).

After 5 minutes, check on the frittata. If the eggs start to be cooked on top and they are well cooked along the edges, it's the perfect time to flip the frittata onto the lid and then slide it gently back into the skillet, to cook the other side for 5 minutes. The trick to a perfect flipping is the cooking point of the top of the frittata.

Let it rest for 5 minutes and then enjoy.

STUFFED TOMATOES

FOR 8 PEOPLE

This is a summer classic that my grandmother used to make at every big festivity, or when she wanted to impress her guests. She always made her own mayonnaise, which can truly make this dish a gourmet one. It can be either an appetizer or an entrée, but try to only make it in the summer, as that's the season when tomatoes are at their best, juicy, ripe, sweet…I am a big fan of eating old-fashioned, respecting the seasons and the beauty they have to offer.

For a vegan version: use chickpeas instead of tuna, and simply skip the eggs.

Preparation: 1 hour or 1½ hours if making homemade mayonnaise

4 large, round tomatoes
¼ cup capers
3 anchovy fillets
3 tbsp. mayonnaise (or to taste)
2 cans of Italian tuna in extra-virgin olive oil
Juice and zest of ½ lemon
2 eggs
Fresh dill, thyme, and parsley to taste
Salt and pepper to taste

Rinse the tomatoes, and cut the tops being careful not to break them, as they will be used for decoration. Gently scoop out the inner part, add some salt and let them drain upside-down while you prepare the filling.

Hard boil two eggs. (Suggested instructions appear on the next page.)

This is a very fun part because you can make your own version of filling. In a mixing bowl, mix the tuna (drained from its olive oil), the mayo, a squeeze of lemon juice, and some zest (to taste).

Finely chop the capers, the herbs, and the anchovies, then add to the tuna mix.
Cut the eggs finely into the mix.

Stir well to combine all the ingredients, then taste, and add salt/lemon/herbs accordingly. You can also add more anchovies if you'd like. This is a very creative recipe that allows you plenty of room to make it yours.

Stuff the tomatoes with the filling, sit down, and enjoy!

MADRI'S RICE SALAD (INSALATA DI RISO)

FOR 6 PEOPLE

This is another classic my grandmother would make weekly. The only ingredient I changed from the original recipe is Vienna sausages[1]. This dish is the perfect summer recipe to take over to a friend for a lunch on the patio—it's the perfect dish for a hot summer night when the last thing you want to do is cooking—it makes a beautiful leftover. And it can also be made in advance; in fact, the rice must be at room temperature when assembling the dish. One more fact: kids love to decorate it and add all the ingredients, at least I did, and Catherine does as well.

Preparation: 15 minutes
Cooking time: 20 minutes
Passive time: 30-40 minutes to cool down

20-30 black olives, pitted
2 tomatoes
150 gr. (5.3 oz.) Emmenthal
7 artichoke hearts in extra-virgin olive oil
3 tbsp. capers
4 eggs
¼ cup cocktail onions
2 cups of basmati rice
4 cornichons
¼ cup baby corn
¼ cup petit green peas
1½ can of Italian tuna in extra-virgin olive oil
1 lemon (zest and juice)
1 tbsp. of mayonnaise and 1 tbsp. of Dijon mustard (optional)
2 tbsp. fresh dill
Salt and pepper to taste

For the eggs:
Place the eggs in a saucepan filled with water. Bring to a boil and cook for 9 minutes from boiling. Remove the eggs and allow to cool down.

For the rice:
Cook rice in salted, boiling water.
When rice has cooked, drain and, in the colander, cool down with running cold water. This passage will prevent rice from overcooking.

---

1 In Italian, we call it Würstel, using the German word.

When the rice has cooled down (must reach room temperature), place in a large salad bowl and add some extra-virgin olive oil to prevent it from sticking. Set aside.

For the salad:
On a cutting board, dice Emmental into small bitesize cubes, do the same with the tomatoes and the baby corn. Add to the rice.

Cut black olives in quarters, dice the artichokes, onions, and the cornichons, then add to the salad as well.

Drain the tuna from the can and break it into flakes. Add to rice.
Add the green peas (previously thawed), fresh dill, salt, freshly ground black pepper, the juice of ½ lemon, and more olive oil.

Gently toss the rice salad and taste. You may need more lemon juice or more oil to taste.
Add the eggs (that you have peeled and cut in quarters) on top of the salad to form the rays of a sun as a decoration.

Allow the salad to chill and marinate for 3-4 hours, then serve.

You can keep this salad in the fridge for up to 3 days.

MADRI'S SEMI-SAUERKRAUT

FOR 4 PEOPLE

This is another classic I remember Madri making. I am not sure this is the exact recipe from my childhood, but it's my version of it and the closest to the one I remember eating with my grandparents.

Preparation: 10 minutes
Cooking time: 20-25 minutes

1 head of green cabbage
Salt, extra-virgin olive oil, and apple cider vinegar to taste
(I start with 1 tsp. and work my way into the sourness I want.)

Shred the cabbage very finely (a mandolin is very useful here if you don't want to use a knife and chopping board).

Sauté the cabbage in extra-virgin olive oil for 10-15 minutes before adding the vinegar and salt.

Cook until browned and nicely caramelized and add as much (or little vinegar) you wish.

Note: I like to add the vinegar when the cabbage is partially cooked because I noticed it absorbs less of it and the vinegar has all the time to evaporate, just like with white wine.

PUMPKIN SOUP
WITH RICE AND MILK

FOR 6–8 PEOPLE

I have mixed memories of this soup. I remember a traditional milk soup from Piemonte, I remember Madri making it, and I remember yellow squash and rice. What I know is that, with this version of one of her magic soups (yes, her soups were legendary) I can travel back in time to elementary school, and then to middle school, when my brother and I would spend one night a week (usually Tuesdays) at my grandparents'. It was our favorite night of the week: We would watch Perry Mason after dinner, and then we would go to bed in a room full of magic (basically clothes and accessories), but I thought they were magical, just like her soups.

Preparation: 15 minutes
Cooking time: 45-60 minutes
Passive time: 10 minutes to cool down

1 medium pumpkin (or kabocha squash, or butternut squash)
1 cup of arborio rice
1.7 fl. oz or 3-4 tbsp. (50 ml.) of your favorite milk
      (*dairy or non-dairy, unsweetened oat milk is the best for this.*)
2 carrots
1 stick of celery
1 leek
1 sprig of fresh thyme
1 sprig of fresh rosemary
A few leaves of sage
Extra-virgin olive oil, a tiny bit of butter, black pepper, and salt to taste

Peel the pumpkin and dice it.

Transfer diced pumpkin into the pressure cooker with the rest of the vegetables (whole) and the herbs. If you have a Parmigiano rind, add it also. Do not add salt or oil at this point. Add the water all the way to the mark on the pot (I like to make extra broth that I can use for other preparations or freeze).

Close the pressure cooker and cook for 15-20 minutes from the whistle. Then, wait until the pressure cooker is silent before opening. If you don't have a pressure cooker, cook the pumpkin and the vegetables in a stockpot until the pumpkin is soft.

Remove the vegetables and 2 cups of pumpkin and broth.

With the immersion blender, puree the 2 cups you have removed, then transfer it back with the rest of the soup. You can use the boiled vegetables for other preparations or, like we used to in my home, eat them with a good mayo.

Add the rice and let it simmer, uncovered, until it's fully cooked.

Add salt to taste and (optionally) drizzle with some extra-virgin olive oil.

Add milk and adjust salt and pepper. Let it rest for 20 minutes before serving with plenty of freshly grated parmesan cheese.

This soup, like most soups, is even better the following day. So, it does make a beautiful leftover, and it can also be frozen. My family is made up of three people, so I often make big batches of soup, and freeze for those days when I don't have time to cook. Both my mother and grandmother were big on freezing food for "those days." The leftover, you'll see, will become almost a risotto, and that's a good thing.

STUFFED BELL PEPPERS

FOR 6–8 PEOPLE

Bell peppers are one of my favorite vegetables, and stuffed bell peppers are delicious, and very versatile. My grandmother used to stuff them with ground meat, usually a mix of pork and beef, but I find that tuna and anchovies make this recipe even better, somewhat recalling the region's traditional dish, *bagna càuda*[2]. Tuna can be easily substituted with more breadcrumbs, capers, cheese, and olives.

Preparation: 20 minutes
Cooking time: 1 hour
Passive time: 10 minutes

4 big bell peppers, 1 for each color, red, yellow, orange and green
        (*or what is available at the market*)
2 tbsp. (20-25 gr.) capers in vinegar, rinsed
1 anchovy fillet (optional)
150 gr. (5.3 oz.) canned tuna in extra-virgin olive oil (drained)
100 gr. (3.5 oz.) of good bread like ciabatta, sourdough, or baguette
Enough milk to cover the bread entirely for soaking
2 tbsp. grated parmesan cheese
1 tbsp. grated pecorino cheese
Fresh parsley, basil, chives, thyme to taste
Extra-virgin olive oil, salt, and pepper to taste
Zest of ½ lemon
1 pinch of palm sugar or brown sugar

Preheat the oven to 375°F.

Cut the tops off the peppers and then cut them in half lengthwise, to create the "container" for the filling. Place bell peppers on a baking sheet and roast in the oven until they begin to soften and slightly brown along the edges (approximately 15-20 minutes).

In a mixing bowl, soak the bread in milk and set aside.

Finely chop the capers and the anchovy fillet; then mix with the tuna.

On a cutting board, finely chop parsley, basil, and thyme, add to the mix. Add pepper and taste Squeeze all the milk out of the bread and add to the tuna, then zest the lemon and add extra-virgin olive oil, herbs, salt, and sugar to taste (be mindful of salt; I often don't add it at all because of the saltiness of capers and anchovies).

---

2 *This is a traditional dish from Piemonte, a sauce of heavy cream, garlic, and anchovies in which cooked and raw vegetables are dipped. The sauce is kept warm by a candle and is traditionally eaten in a terracotta bowl.*

Remove bell peppers from the oven, sprinkle a few salt flakes (or regular salt), and drizzle with extra-virgin olive oil, then carefully fill them with the tuna mix. Use a spoon and remember they're hot. Cover with aluminum foil to create moisture, and to prevent the filling from drying up (tuna tends to do so).

Lower the oven temperature to 300°F and bake for 10 more minutes. Turn off the oven and let it rest for 15 minutes with its door closed. I love when bell peppers cook slowly, at low heat; the filling gently releases its flavor at its best, deep into the soft bell peppers.
Serve warm, or even better the day after.

WINTER WONDERLAND
SAVORY GALETTE

FOR 4–6 PEOPLE

I love how forgiving a galette is, and every time you make the crust you become more comfortable with baking it, and with achieving a perfect dry (not soggy) bottom. One day, you'll wake up and it will be one of your go-to's for dessert or, like in this case, as a main dish that everybody will love, including kids. This, in fact, is a great way to have your kids eat broccoli, that has never tasted better before.

Preparation: 20 minutes
Cooking time: 35-40 minutes
Passive time: 30 minutes for the dough to rest in the fridge

Ingredients for the dough:

250 gr. (8.8 oz.) all-purpose flour
140 gr. (4.9 oz.) ripe sourdough starter (chilled)
1 stick unsalted butter, cold
¼ tsp. of salt
1 tsp. iced water or more, if necessary
1 egg for the egg wash

Ingredients for the filling:

1 cup broccoli florets
½ cup cauliflower florets (*I love yellow cauliflower*)
1 small red onion
2 small potatoes
2 leeks
Stilton cheese to taste
½ cup pecans or walnuts
1 tbsp. crème fraîche
Extra-virgin olive oil, salt, and pepper to taste

Making the dough:

In a food processor, pulse flour, salt, and cold butter (cubed) until it crumbles.

Add the chilled sourdough starter and the iced water and pulse until the mix comes together. It does so in no time, and it's important not to overwork the dough.

Pour the mix onto a pastry board and work the dough until it all comes together. Form a disk and cover in plastic wrap.

Chill the dough in the fridge for at least an hour; you can make this dough in advance and chill overnight before using it. You can freeze the dough up to three months. If you do freeze it, thaw it in the fridge overnight before use.

Making the filling:

Rinse broccoli and cauliflower, cut into small florets, and steam for 5 minutes.

Move them to an ice bath to preserve color and texture.

Remove the tops from the leeks, as well as the first three layers of the vegetable; slice them finely with a mandolin, and do the same with the red onion, then sauté in extra-virgin olive oil until golden.

Add the broccoli and the cauliflower and sauté for 5 minutes, then set aside and allow to cool down.

Slice the potatoes very finely and chop the nuts.

Sprinkle the nuts all over the crust, then cover with plastic wrap and roll out the dough until you form a 20-inch disk. Half-way through the rolling process, move the crust to a silicon mat that you will place onto the round baking dish; this will make the transfer much easier when the crust starts to be thin.

Puncture the crust with a fork, then spread the crème fraîche all over the crust. Now layer the thin potatoes, then cover with the veggies.

Top with as much crumbled Stilton as you wish and fold the edges of the galette.
Beat the egg in a small bowl and brush the entirety of the crust with an egg wash. Brush inside the small creases as well, as this will help seal any possible little hole you may have.

Bake at 400°F for 35-40 minutes or until the dough is nicely golden brown and the filling bubbly and shiny.

Allow to cool down for 5-10 minutes and enjoy.

BREADSTICK SOUP
FOR BREAKFAST

A few weeks ago, Catherine and I had breakfast outside, on the patio. We used to do this every day, until June gloom arrived, and we felt more comfortable inside at the kitchen table.

When we had our breakfast, that morning, June gloom had not shown up.

"It's not foggy!" Catherine said as soon as I opened the shutters, in her bedroom, when I woke her up. "There is the sun! *C'è il sole!*" She was so happy that she decided not to read the usual morning books; she wanted to go down to the kitchen, spread some honey on her *fette biscottate*[3].

So, we set the table, sat down, and began to eat.

The breeze brushed my hair. "It feels like the end of summer in Pilaz," I thought.

My heart got heavy, all of a sudden, heavy with a sense of longing. Pilaz is a small village in the Aosta Valley, in Italy, where I spent all my childhood summer and winter vacations.

While Catherine ate, I started to type this in my notes, on my phone. I try not to stay too much on the phone in front of her, since we are limiting screen time to a minimum (Skype with my parents, Ben's sisters, and Mr. Rogers in the evening).

"*Mamma deve solo scrivere una cosa amore*, OK?" I told her. Mama just needs to write something down, my love.

The wind chimes that hang just behind the table sounded like the church bells from the nearby town of Antagnod, just a few minutes up the hill from Pilaz. I could almost see the yellow dome of the bell tower, the small, beautiful cemetery right below, and the mountains.

The color of the sky, that morning in Los Angeles, was intense; not quite blue, not quite gray—magical. It was as if, like at the end of summer up in the mountains, it held back the rain just a little longer.

I dipped a *fetta biscottata* in my latte, no sugar, just a splash of oat milk. In Pilaz, breakfast was simple as well, made of *grissini soup* (breadsticks dipped in warm caffe latte). Just two houses up from ours, Marco Perono, the town baker, made the best breadsticks I have ever had to

---

3 *A traditional breakfast item that is very common in Italy: a crunchy semi-sweet toast on which honey, marmalade, or butter are spread.*

this day. They are special, because they are made with the iced water that comes straight from the mountains, a water like no other.

When I was little, I always wanted one of Marco's breadsticks and a roof stalactite (something you could grab from any roof back in the days, when rain was still relatively pure water). My grandmother would wrap the ice in a paper towel, and I would take a bite of each. I remember being happy, and I remember the feeling of holding the ice in my hands, and the flavor of that odd combination.

I tell Catherine I am writing about Pilaz. She wants to go there and see the cows.

We keep eating; I look at the view. I see Griffith Park, and the massive oak tree in my garden. The wind blows, the sun comes out a little more. In Pilaz, we had breakfast at the tiny kitchen table by the window where we saw the mountains, the main street to Champoluc, the bigger town just a few minutes away, and the Èvançon stream across the street. When I was little, there wasn't much traffic.

I would face my grandparents; behind me a cabinet where we kept oil, sugar, and salt, behind them a poster with all the species of mushrooms. The setting was perfect for us all to look outside.

Our kitchen window stood by the balcony where Anna, the owner of the house and my grandmother's best friend, would hang clothes to dry.

She would come up every morning to wish the *bun levà*, good morning in the Aosta Valley patuà (dialect). My grandmother wouldn't start her day well without Anna's good morning.

The water of the Èvançon stream is a unique shade of blue and gray.

When I was little, in fact for my first 18 years of life, we spent the month of August in Pilaz, because my grandparents rented a beautiful house there. They had started renting in 1982, the year I was born, and my grandfather kept the house until 2002, one year after my grandmother died.

Every now and then, I read a few pages of my grandmother's diaries. But I haven't done it in a while, so I decided to take the opportunity given me by this piece for opening one up and see, out of curiosity, what she wrote of a normal day in August, in Pilaz.

It was cloudy and it rained on August 5th of 1989; it was a Saturday.

I read that I had breakfast alone with my grandmother, and that after we had finished, we went downstairs to wish Anna good morning. We went to the nearby town of Periasc to buy some groceries, and on the way back we walked home through the pine forest along which the Èvançon stream runs. After lunch, we walked to the trout lake and ate our afternoon snack there. The following day, my brother and I woke up very early and went into my grandparents' bed for cuddles. That same evening, we went on a walk with my mom, before retiring for the day.

I could read her stories forever. Her writing isn't erudite. And yet every word opens up a world. Every word refreshes my memory, almost as if I could clearly remember 1989.

I don't have many regrets. I took many wrong turns over the years, and I would avoid some of them if I could. Maybe my biggest regret is never having been able to tell my grandparents how much I loved them, how much I appreciated them, and that my most vivid and powerful memories are of the stories I created with them.

Some of my most vivid memories are about the end of summer in Pilaz, and of the long shadows approaching, as Anna calls that time of year.

Thank you, Madri and Nonno.

PASTA

ZEN SPAGHETTI
AND MEATBALLS

2012 is when I first walked into the Los Angeles Rinzai-ji Zen Center, where my Zen practice had started, just a few months before meeting Leonard Cohen in New York.

It had been a rough year: I was trying to stay sober, I was having an affair with a married man I was desperately in love with, and I had debts to pay. My writing career had come to a halt. I was so broken that I was ready to leave everything behind to follow the Zen path.

I didn't know much about Zen the first time I went to the zendo on Cimarron Street, quite far from Hollywood, where I lived at the time. I knew that Leonard had studied there with Joshu Sasaki Roshi, that he had been ordained, and that he had lived at the Mt. Baldy center for a while. In those days I was in pain, and Leonard's story of discovering Zen practice had inspired me. I didn't have anything to lose, so I gave it a try, hoping it would do me some good.

The first time I went was on a Sunday morning. I remember that day with nostalgia, but also with profound joy, and gratitude. I haven't thought about that day in a long time.

In those days, my friend Tomas let me use his car, a red Camaro, in exchange for babysitting his two kids. I would park the giant car one block away from the building because I was shy, and I didn't feel comfortable using the Zen center's parking lot. The neighborhood wasn't very safe, but some of the most beautiful Victorian houses I had ever seen framed the naked and almost deserted intersection at 25th Avenue and Cimarron Street. Even if most of them could have benefitted from a massive remodel, their regal austerity had not lost character and charm. It didn't take me long to feel at ease walking on the streets around the temple, empty—other than for a few kids riding their bikes—and an ice cream truck that played La Cucaracha and White Christmas all year long.

I met Koyo there. He was the head monk at the time—tall, thin, ageless.

I was very shy, and for weeks I did not talk to anyone at the temple. But one day, after zazen, I was so sad and in pain that I talked to Koyo.

He had listened and given me answers that nobody else had given me before: "Sometimes, all we have to do is survive, sweetheart," he had said. I didn't understand Zen, but I didn't have to. I kept going back, and I began to feel better.

One day, I had asked Koyo if there was anything I could do to be of service. He had helped me so much that I wanted to give back and get more involved in the daily activities of the center.

"Well, you are Italian—could you make spaghetti and meatballs?" Koyo had said as he helped me fold the last of many black robes back in the closet.

That's how the Friday night dinners started.

Friday after Friday, new friends moved into the Zen center, and they brought with them their own light, their own darkness, and their own recipes. The kitchen on Cimarron Street had become my favorite place in the world.

It was fantastic!

I can still hear the laughter, the smells, the sweet and tangy taste of the tomato sauce, the soft ground meat blending in with onions, parsley, garlic, and lots of parmesan cheese.

Every week we'd try a different dish with the ingredients we could find at the farmers' market, and with what the monks had in the fridge. We'd prepare appetizers, pastas, salads, fish, and always dessert. I remember dicing celery and onion slowly, with the same grace I tried to master when pouring the tea at the end of our evening meditation. The blade cutting through the transparency of the vegetables was an extension of my arm, and through it I could feel every layer, the crunch, and ultimately the cut. In the kitchen I was relaxed, and I performed every movement with a natural rhythm.

The kitchen on Cimarron Street was spacious and open onto the dining hall on one side, and onto the garden on another. Pans, pots, and tools were old, not state of the art, and yet the room itself looked just like a restaurant's: There was a big gas stove, a spacious island in the middle, one big freezer, and two fridges with plenty of gourmet leftovers for the nights when we weren't there, when dinner for monks and students was usually made of soup, tofu, and vegetables.

The double sink could hold almost all the dishes and the pots, so there was room for three of us sharing the washing ritual: 1) soap, 2) water, and 3) towel. I loved witnessing how the kitchen warmed up, cooled down, and shone again. The kitchen was just a continuation of the sitting, of the chanting, and of the walking meditation we practiced before dinner. For the first time, I experienced how Zen practice could reflect into daily life, and how the meditative state of mind naturally merged into cooking.

One day Koyo left. He was suddenly moved to a temple in Colorado. I was devastated.

"Sometimes, all we have to do is survive, sweetheart," he had said.

I did survive. And I still talk to Koyo.

ORECCHIETTE WITH BROCCOLI RABE

FOR 4 PEOPLE

This is my grandmother Maddalena's recipe. She was born in a small town near Bari, in Puglia, and moved to Avigliana[4], near Turin—where I was born and raised—shortly after the Second World War, when many southerners were moving north to find work. My father was 5 years old; it was 1948.

Preparation: 10-15 minutes
Cooking time: 15 minutes

320 gr. (11.3 oz.) orecchiette pasta
2 bunches of broccoli rabe (rapini)
Extra-virgin olive oil to taste
Salt to taste
2 cloves of garlic, whole
Crushed red pepper flakes to taste (optional)

Rinse and clean the broccoli rabe. Select good leaves and the florets (I love the leaves).
Bring a large pot of water to a boil over high heat. Salt the water when it starts to boil and blanch the rapini for 2-3 minutes.

Drain the greens (save the water) and pour them in a sautéing pan or a skillet with extra-virgin olive oil and 2 cloves of garlic, whole.

Sauté for 5 minutes, remove from heat and set aside, covered.

Bring the water back to a boil and cook the orecchiette al dente.

Drain pasta al dente and transfer to the skillet with the broccoli rabe. Sauté to allow the flavors to come together, remove garlic, and serve with some red pepper flakes (optional).

---

4 *Avigliana is a beautiful and historic small town 30 minutes from Turin. Avigliana is famous for its two beautiful lakes, and for its history, having a strategic position between France and Italy.*

CREAMY BUTTERNUT SQUASH BUCATINI

FOR 4 PEOPLE

As I recovered from my bulimia, it was important for me to make and eat food I enjoyed. I was done with just enduring it. So, all my food, in a way, had been a journey to this very recipe (and the one that follows); they are two examples of what I consider comfort food. On the show and on Instagram we often discuss the difference between junk food and comfort food, and these two examples perfectly describe what culinary comfort means to me: a warm embrace.

Preparation: 15 minutes
Cooking time 1 hour

1 medium butternut squash
2 leeks
¼ onion
2 leaves of sage
1 clove of garlic
300 gr. (10.6 oz.) of bucatini
2-3 cups vegetable broth or water
¼ cup of parmigiano cheese
Extra-virgin olive oil, salt, pepper, and butter to taste

Peel the butternut squash and chop it into small cubes.
Clean the leeks and chop them very finely.

Transfer leeks and butternut squash to a pot with extra-virgin olive oil, the clove of garlic, and a small amount of butter, then sauté for a minute or two; enjoy the smell.

Add sage and vegetable broth, lower heat, and cover with a lid.

Cook until the butternut squash is soft, stirring occasionally so it doesn't stick to the bottom of the pot (this takes approximately 20 minutes).

Break the bucatini into 2-inch pieces and add to the butternut squash. Add a small amount of water if needed to cook the pasta, but not too much or this will turn into a soup.

Cover with the lid and cook, stirring regularly. The gluten from the pasta will create a beautiful creaminess.

When the pasta is cooked, usually 10 minutes or so, it will have absorbed most of the water; it's now time to add the Parmigiano.

Stir, cook for 5 more minutes, and serve warm.

CREAMY CAULIFLOWER PASTA

FOR 4 PEOPLE

This pasta will taste even better than mac 'n' cheese. Just like the one before, this is a perfect example of comfort food that is not junk food. The cauliflower is so versatile that you can play with spices adding perhaps some smoked paprika instead of nutmeg, and you can use yellow cauliflower for an even more delicate flavor. I also made it with purple cauliflower, and the bright purple turned into a pastel pink when cooked in water. Catherine loved eating "pink pasta."

Preparation: 15 minutes
Cooking time 1 hour

1 head of cauliflower
1 leek
½ onion
2 leaves of sage
1 small sprig of rosemary and 1 of thyme, (chopped if you want a stronger flavor or whole for a milder one); you will remove the herbs before serving, in this case
1 clove of garlic
1 pinch of nutmeg
250 gr. (8.8 oz.) elbow pasta or short pasta
2-3 cups vegetable broth or water
½ cup Parmigiano cheese
Extra-virgin olive oil, salt, pepper, and butter to taste

Thoroughly rinse the cauliflower and cut it into small florets.

Clean the leeks and the onion, then chop them very finely.

Transfer leeks, onion, and cauliflower to a pot with extra-virgin olive oil, the clove of garlic, and a small amount of butter, then sauté for a minute or two.

Add herbs and vegetable broth, lower the heat, and cover with a lid.

Cook until the cauliflower is soft, stirring occasionally so it doesn't stick to the bottom of the pot. (This takes approximately 20 minutes).

Throw the pasta in and add a small amount of water if needed to cook it, but not too much or this will turn into a soup.

Cover with the lid and cook, stirring regularly. The gluten from the pasta will create a beautiful creaminess.

When the pasta is cooked, usually 10 minutes or so, it will have absorbed most of the water, and it is now time to add the Parmigiano.

Stir, cook for 5 more minutes, and serve warm.

SOFFRITTO PASTA

Soffritto is the base of many Italian dishes, originally made of sautéed carrots, celery, and onion, diced, and cooked in extra-virgin olive oil until the onions (or shallot) become translucent. It is customary to add, at this point, the main ingredients: Meat, rice, vegetables. Usually, soffritto is not the main ingredient of a dish, but it is so good that I decided to change things.

At every show, every time I would make a soffritto, I loved the scent so much that I would always say: "Guys, this is so good you could just eat it as is or make a pasta with it." So, I finally made a pasta with it and the result was even better than I had imagined.

What I also love about this pasta, is that we all have the ingredients in the fridge to make it. Which pasta to use is up to you, but I would suggest egg pasta like pappardelle or tagliatelle, because they are very porous and remind me of Bolognese ragú, for which soffritto is the base.

Preparation: 10 minutes
Cooking time: 15-20 minutes

350 gr. (12.4 oz.) fresh egg pasta like tagliatelle or pappardelle
6 small carrots
4 small leeks or 2 small onions
2 cloves of garlic
1 pinch of palm sugar or brown sugar
Extra-virgin olive oil, salt, pepper, white wine, and Parmigiano cheese to taste

Rinse all the vegetables and chop them very finely but keep the clove of garlic whole because we will remove it.

Sauté all the vegetables in extra-virgin olive oil until nice and caramelized. Salt to taste, add the pinch of palm sugar and, last, add a tablespoon or so of white wine. Cook for 5 more minutes for the wine to evaporate, then remove the garlic and set aside.

Cook the pasta al dente in salted boiling water, then drain and add to soffritto.

Add some oil, and sauté for a few minutes before serving with a generous amount of freshly grated Parmigiano cheese.

CREAMY PASTA WITH LEEKS

FOR 4 PEOPLE

This pasta closes the circle of the creamy pastas. I still remember the first time I made it: it was lunch on a Saturday, and leeks were the last vegetable I had in the fridge.

Something that was meant to be a quick lunch with whatever was left in the fridge turned out to be some of the most delicious pasta I had ever had, and it was also one of the latest additions to this book.

Preparation: 5 minutes
Cooking time: 15 minutes

5 leeks
320 gr. (11.3 oz.) fresh pasta, such as *trofie*
2 tbsp. almond ricotta[5] (I like to use Kite Hill)
Salt, pepper, and extra-virgin olive oil to taste

Slice the leeks with a mandolin and sauté in extra-virgin olive oil.

Cook the pasta al dente.

Salt the leeks, transfer most of them to the glass of an immersion blender, add a ladle of cooking water from the pasta, and blend until creamy.

Sauté the cream of leeks with the almond ricotta, then add the pasta, sauté for 5 more minutes and top with the leeks you have set aside. If you need, add some more cooking water from the pasta, as the gluten will help create a very creamy consistency.

Sprinkle some grated pecorino cheese on top and serve right away.

---

5 *I like almond ricotta because it's lighter than dairy ricotta, and because it has a lovely tang that works beautifully with creamy sauces.*

PASTA PRIMAVERA

FOR 4 PEOPLE

Two things I love the most about this simple pasta: the first one is the colorful rainbow of flavor, and the second one is that you can personalize with any spring and summer vegetables you have. For example, you can add fresh peas, mushrooms, bell peppers, spring onions, and even fresh corn. All these pasta recipes are, to me, a beautiful exercise in training our senses, our taste, and our creativity to serve us, give us a good meal and, ultimately, a good life.

Preparation: 15-20 minutes
Cooking time: 20-25 minutes

320 gr. (11.3 oz.) penne pasta
4 fresh asparagus
1 zucchini
1 carrot
3 tbsp. capers, finely chopped
15 Mediterranean olives, choose fresh ones, not canned
5-6 leaves fresh basil
½ ripe tomato (or 1, if small)
30 gr. (1 oz.) flat green beans (or haricot vert)
1 clove garlic
Salt, extra-virgin olive oil, pepper, and chili flakes to taste

Clean the green beans by removing both ends. Rinse well and blanch them by boiling them in salted water for 5 minutes. Drain and give them an ice bath. Drain from iced water, and pat dry. Chop them and set aside.

Chop the zucchini, the asparagus, and the carrots, then start sautéing in extra-virgin olive oil and one clove of garlic (whole). I cut the vegetables quite small, bite-size.

Meanwhile, finely chop the capers and the olives.

After 5 minutes, when carrots and zucchini start to soften, add the green beans, the capers, and the olives.

Sauté for 5 minutes and add salt to taste.

Cook the pasta al dente in salted boiling water.
Remove the garlic, chop the half tomato, and add with the pasta into the skillet. Add the chopped basil, also. Sauté for a few minutes and serve hot.

Note: *If you love capers, like I do, feel free to add more.*

FREGOLA SARDA WITH SNAP PEAS

FOR 4 PEOPLE

Fregola is small spheric pasta made by hand from semolina. This pasta is traditional from Sardinia and it's traditionally served with fresh clams and grated bottarga.

This vegetarian version has a beautiful texture thanks to the chewiness of the fregola and to the crunchiness of the slightly cooked snap peas. You can serve as is or add a spoonful of fresh ricotta at the bottom of the dish.

Preparation: 10-15 minutes
Cooking time 20 minutes

250 gr. (8.8 oz.) fregola sarda
17 oz. (500 gr.) fresh snap peas
1 carrot
1 stick of celery
¼ onion
5 white mushrooms
1 tbsp. (a splash) of white wine
Pecorino cheese (grated), to taste
fresh herbs to taste (optional)

To start, clean the snap peas, rinse them thoroughly, and remove both ends and the thread along the shell, which would be unpleasant to eat.

Prepare a basic soffritto by dicing finely the carrot, the celery, and the onion and sautéing them in extra-virgin olive oil. When they are cooked and the onion is translucent (5-10 minutes), deglaze with white wine and mushrooms (add white wine and allow to evaporate).

Cook the fregola al dente in salted boiling water, like you would do for pasta.

Quickly sauté the snap peas with the soffritto and, when ready, add the fregola.

Sauté for 5 minutes, add salt and pepper to taste, more oil if necessary, and serve with freshly grated pecorino cheese.

THE AUTHENTIC PASTA AND FAGIOLI (PASTA WITH BEANS)

FOR 4 PEOPLE

This is it, the one and only *pasta and fagioli*, pasta with beans. Easy, delicious, earthy, filling, healthy and decadent at the same time. The essence of Italy in a plate, that also happens to freeze beautifully and make an amazing leftover. I am partial, I love beans, but this is a dish you will like even if you're not a bean-head like me.

Preparation: 15 minutes
Cooking time: 15-20 minutes + 20-25 if using dry beans

320 gr. (11.3 oz.) short pasta
Your favorite beans, either canned or dry. If using dry beans, soak them for at least 6
        hours (recipe for basic beans follows). If canned, use 1 can.
1 carrot
1 leek
1 clove of garlic (whole)
1 tomato or 1 cup of tomato sauce
Extra-virgin olive oil, salt, rosemary, pepper, and chili flakes to taste

Cook the beans if you have chosen to use dry ones (I cook them in the pressure cooker for 15 minutes after soaking them overnight). In the pressure cooker I put: 1 carrot, 1 onion, 1 celery stick, 1 spring of rosemary, 1 bay leaf, 1 clove of garlic, and a diced tomato. Or you can choose canned beans to add after all the aromatics are cooked.

If you don't have a pressure cooker, use a stockpot. It will take a little longer, but it won't change the result.

Dice the vegetables, finely chop the aromatics, and sauté in extra-virgin olive oil for 5-8 minutes.

Add beans and either chopped tomato or tomato sauce to the vegetables and sauté for 5 minutes.

Cook pasta al dente in boiling, salted water, and add some of the cooking water to the beans to help create a nice sauce. Remove garlic.

Add pasta to beans and vegetables, mix well and serve with plenty of parmesan cheese on top.

Chili flakes are optional, but I love them.

BUCATINI WITH TOMATO AND CAPERS

FOR 4 PEOPLE

I like to call this the sexy pasta. Sexy because it's peppery, acidic, salty, addictive, and very light without sacrificing taste. Because if you are having a romantic night, you really don't want to eat something heavy that makes you want to go to bed right after dinner.

I love capers, I love olives, I love anchovies. All these ingredients create bold flavors without being heavy on the stomach. Very Italian, very sensual, very intriguing.

Preparation: 10 minutes
Cooking time: 15 minutes

320 gr. (11.3 oz.) bucatini pasta
10 olives, pitted
2 tbsp. capers
1 cup tomato sauce (See recipe on page 179 for my own tomato sauce)
1 tsp. fennel seed
2 anchovies
Extra-virgin olive oil, salt, pepper, garlic, and chili flakes to taste

Finely chop the capers, olives, and anchovies.

In a skillet, with extra-virgin olive oil, sauté tomato sauce for a few minutes, then add the fennel seed, the capers, and the olives. Add olives and garlic.

Cook the pasta al dente.

Drain pasta and add to the sauce.

Sauté for a few minutes and add chili flakes.

PASTA WITH TUNA

FOR 4 PEOPLE

This pasta is the ultimate go-to when in a hurry, especially during summer, when tomatoes are ripe, and the heat pulls us away from the stove.

Preparation: 10 minutes
Cooking time: 10 minutes

320 gr. (11.3 oz.) short pasta (*I love penne with this*)
3 cans of Italian tuna in extra-virgin olive oil
15-20 cherry tomatoes
3 tbs. of capers (drained from the vinegar, but not rinsed)
10 green olives, pitted
Extra-virgin olive oil, salt, pepper, dill to taste

In a large and pretty serving bowl, mix the tuna with the olive oil, and with a fork break it, until it crumbles.

Coarsely chop the tomatoes and add to the tuna. Coarsely chop olives and capers and add as well. Now add fresh dill and more olive oil, if necessary. Allow the tuna to soften, and all these Mediterranean flavors beautifully come together.

Meanwhile, cook pasta in boiling and salted water. Pour some of the cooking water (¼ cup) to the tuna mix.

When al dente, drain the pasta and stir into the tuna mix.

Top pasta with some fresh dill.

STROZZAPRETI PASTA WITH WHITE MUSHROOMS, RACLETTE CHEESE, AND KABOCHA SQUASH

FOR 4 PEOPLE

This dish is comforting and delicious, a recipe that reminds me of something you could order at the restaurant of mountain chalet, and your guests will never believe it takes less than one hour to make. I like to use Kabocha squash because of its creaminess, but you can use butternut squash instead, and it will work just fine. Strozzapreti is a kind of fresh pasta without eggs, interestingly chewy on the outside, but with a core that perfectly stays al dente. The name "strozzapreti" literally means "priests stranglers". One of the legends say that where this pasta is originally from, Emilia Romagna, part of the former Papal State, in Italy, priests loved it so much and had such a voracious appetite that they would eat too much of it, and too fast, to the point of almost choking.

Preparation: 10 minutes
Cooking time: 35-40 minutes

320 gr. (11.3 oz.) strozzapreti pasta (if you can't find strozzapreti, trofie pasta work great, or pretty much any tubular pasta like penne, ziti, or rigatoni)
1lb. of white mushrooms
½ small kabocha squash
200 gr. (7 oz.) of raclette cheese or asiago cheese
½ cup Parmigiano cheese
3 tbsp. of milk or cream
extra-virgin olive oil, salt, and pepper to taste

Cut the kabocha in a half, remove the seeds, and bake at 425°F until soft but not overcooked, approximately 30 minutes.

Meanwhile, prepare the cheese by dicing it.

Clean the mushrooms, cut into quarters, and sauté them in extra-virgin olive oil, salt, and pepper. Cook the pasta in salted boiling water and drain when al dente.

At this point, the kabocha should be ready. Take it out of the oven but keep the oven on. Dice half of the kabocha and remove the peel.

Take a baking dish and stir together the pasta, the mushrooms and the kabocha and 2-3 tablespoons of milk or cream.

Salt and pepper to taste, add the cheese, mix well, and grate some Parmigiano on top. Bake the pasta at 425°F for 10-15 minutes and serve.

WHEN I WAS CHUBBY:
THE ITALIAN SUMMER OF 1997

from 2020

have been thinking about the memory of summer a lot lately, maybe because—believe it or not—summer is approaching. In quarantine, I feel as if our perception of time has changed.

One afternoon in May 2020, I visited with my friend Tessa. We hadn't seen each other in a while and so we decided to put our masks on and have a socially distant visit. As I waited at one traffic light, on my way to her house, "Foo Fighter's Next Year" played on the radio.

"Do you remember when, at the end of summer, you could only dream about the summer to come, the following year?" I thought, in Italian. *"Ti ricordi quando, alla fine dell'estate, l'unica cosa che sognavi era l'estate prossima?"*

Then the song ended, and I focused on the street.

I didn't realize that, when I had asked myself that simple question, I had gone quite deep into the answer with my memory. I would long for next summer to come, with the sun of the summer now ending still burning my skin.

The day went by; I saw my friend, bought some food, and returned home.

The morning after, May 21, exactly one month before the beginning of summer 2020, I woke up, picked up Catherine from her crib, watched the garbage trucks drive by (big event every Thursday over here), and prepared breakfast, the usual: golden rusks (fette biscottate) with honey.

Catherine and I sat at the table on the patio and enjoyed our breakfast. Like most mornings, she wanted to listen to Lucio Battisti, a legendary Italian songwriter.

"Acqua Azzurra, mamma," Catherine asked; it's her favorite song of his, a classic.

So, we listened to it, while eating the crunchy rusks; I like to dip mine in my *caffè latte*, she likes to leave traces of honey everywhere.

"This is my favorite breakfast," I thought, looking at the back of Griffith Park, my view from the garden. It was a beautiful spring morning.

Fette biscottate with *caffè latte* is one of the most popular (and simple) Italian everyday breakfasts.

I miss Italy.

Since I moved to the United States, I have never let more than one year go by without returning home, and this time, because of Covid-19, it's the longest I have been away. I miss Italy in the summer the most; the last time I spent the warm season there was 2008.

The song ended, Catherine ate a few slices of banana and a mulberry, while another classic played on my Lucio Battisti playlist: 7 e 40.

Come on a walk down memory lane with me, will you?

When I was 15 and 16, my mom and I vacationed for 2 weeks in Viserba, a small Italian town in the region of Emilia Romagna. It is close to Rimini, a popular summer destination of the Romagna Riviera (riviera romagnola) on the Adriatic Sea.

My father worked I guess, and my younger brother was probably at baseball summer camp...I don't recall why they weren't there.

This is one of the sweetest and most cherished memories I have with my mom, even though my mom and I had an argument while I was writing this essay, because we disagreed on the exact location of the hotel.

For two years in a row, in 1997 and 1998, we took the train from Torino to Viserba (near Rimini), and we would stay at the Hotel Monterosa, on Via G. Dati, 8.

We didn't have much money, the hotel wasn't fancy, and yet it is, to this day, one of the warmest places I remember staying at (and I had the blessing of staying in some of the most beautiful hotels in the world, thanks to Ben). While writing this piece, out of curiosity, I did some research: the hotel has been remodeled, and it is now called La Morosa (dialect for "the girlfriend").

The riviera embodies the essence of a classic Italian summer: crowded beaches, tourists returning year after year, same rented umbrella, and chair, only one, for my mom (I would lay on the sand). Same spot, same ice cream kiosk, same everything—what made it special, the feeling of home.

"Cocco bello, cocco fresco!" would scream the coconut man slaloming between umbrellas and chaise lounges selling slices of fresh coconut.

On my CD player I'd listen to Alanis Morissette.

But let me get to the point, because you know there is more to this than an Italian beach in the month of July.

Picture this: I am 15, chubby, cool AF, I would say now, but looking back…not so much what I would be thinking of myself in the years to come. I have cut my hair short like Natalie Imbruglia. The style doesn't suit me, but when I look at myself in the mirror, I like myself.

I love Kurt Cobain, and with my best friend Paola, I wear distressed jeans with Doc Martens. In the evenings, I eat peppermint and *puffo* (Smurf) gelato with my mom as we stroll along the promenade watching painters making cool art with spray paint. Everybody walks in the evening, showing off golden tan and long legs. The smell of after sun lotion is strong, my favorite scent of summer. Women wear mini-skirts, and little make up because of the beautiful, sexy, tan men walk proud and relaxed in their linen pants.

I have the biggest crush on Alessandro, the son of the managers of the *Hotel Monterosa*, Loretta and Paolo.

He is skinny, cool, has a James Dean look. He likes me, as a friend, and he is 21.

I didn't get it, back then.

I thought it was because I wasn't thin.

Maybe that was also the reason, but I was 15, he was 21.

I didn't get it.

To go back to the song that Catherine and I listened to while having *fette biscottate* with honey, "7 e 40", that song was Alessandro's favorite, or at least one I remember him playing a lot on his guitar. Of course, he played guitar!

At the end of our vacation, when I had to return to Torino with my mom, I would start the countdown to the next summer, when I would see "my love" again. I hoped he would wait for me. I wrote him letters. I'd count the days to see him again…and then life changed. My memory is now blurred.

I thought it was because I wasn't thin. So, I became thin, thinner, and thinner. But Alessandro never knew.

I smile now, with tenderness and compassion, looking back. I look at that Alice, the last Alice before the starving, the throwing up, the cutting, the drugs, the drinks, the sex. I look at that Alice and I aspire to go back to her pure heart, to her unbleached bright spirit, to that Alice before the Alice of blurred and missing memories.

I love that these images, for me, come up with music and food, Italian songs and *fette biscottate* with honey...

Here's some of the food that reminds me of that Alice and a few songs of those years, the late '90s, when everything changed, and yet when everything stayed frozen for me to thaw and retrieve right now, when I can enjoy it to its fullest.

Food:
- Peppermint and Smurf gelato in a cone (vanilla gelato with blue
  food coloring, but it tastes better than vanilla because it's blue)
- Savory breakfast at the hotel buffet, sliced cheese,
  and sliced prosciutto
- ESTATHE lemon iced tea
- Piadina romagnola
- Deep-fried calamari with lemon wedges

Songs:
- I'll Be Missing You — Puff Daddy ft. Faith Evans
- Bittersweet Symphony — The Verve
- Confusa e Felice — Carmen Consoli
- Frozen — Madonna
- Torn — Natalie Imbruglia

COOKIES

COOKIES

During the Covid-19 lockdown, like pretty much the rest of the world, I baked. Without planning it, I created a whole series of cookies that are unique, healthy, irresistible, and mostly vegan-friendly. I started to experiment with the use of nut flours, nut milks, and nut oils. I didn't do it for health reasons, I did it out of curiosity. I think that—in a time of insecurity, fear, monotony and isolation, my creativity found in these cookies the perfect medium. I had fun creating them; I gave countless batches to my neighbors, friends, and kept several for me, Ben, and Catherine.

They are so good that I thought about selling them. But a global pandemic wasn't the best time to start a food business, so I decided to share the recipes in this book.

HAZELNUT AND ESPRESSO COOKIES

FOR 10 COOKIES

If you have ever travelled on an Italian highway, you know that *Autogrill*[6] (a chain of highway rest stops) is one of the finest restaurants on the road; rest stop, in fact, doesn't do it justice. *Autogrill* is an institution, something that every Italian loves, whether for their coffee, jam-filled croissant, licorice candy (*rotelle*), or paninis. From basic to regional and creative, their menu is always comforting, something that reminds you where you are: on the road, on your way to the beach driving from the north to the south, or simply heading somewhere. Heading somewhere is always exciting, and *Autogrill* has always been, at least for me, synonymous with excitement. These cookies, because of their strong cappuccino aroma, reminded me of *Autogrill* even before I tasted them. They are unique, one of my favorites, and something that—on your next trip to Italy—I am sure you will remember.

Cooking time: 10 minutes
Passive time: 10 minutes

150 gr. (5.3 oz.) hazelnut flour
100 gr. (3.5 oz.) all-purpose flour
50 gr. (1.8 oz.) potato starch
75 gr. (2.6 oz.) sugar
2 tbsp. (20 ml.) coffee (*I used leftovers from my morning coffee, but you can make espresso for it, and wait until it cools down.*)
¼ tbsp. baking powder
1 tbsp. (15 gr.) raw unsweetened baking cocoa
1 pinch of salt
1 tbsp. (10 gr.) espresso powder
2.8 fl. oz. (80 ml.) hazelnut oil
(*or your favorite vegetable baking oil, I love almond or canola*).
¼ tsp. vanilla extract
2 tbsp. (20 ml.) buttermilk or unsweetened almond milk

In a mixing bowl, mix all the dry ingredients together.

Add the coffee, the buttermilk (or the almond milk), the oil, and the vanilla extract.

Form ten patties, like you would do for a burger.

Bake for 10 minutes at 425°F.

---

6 *Autogrill is an Italian-based, multinational catering company that is present on most highway reststops all over the country.*

ITALIAN COCONUT
AND LEMON COOKIES

FOR 10 COOKIES

These cookies, one of my latest experiments, reminded me of my paternal grandmother, Maddalena. She would always buy cookies with a similar flavor from an old woman at the market of Avigliana, the small town near Torino (Turin) where I was raised. The market happens every Thursday, in Piazza del Popolo[7], the main town square. I don't remember the name of the woman, but I remember exactly what she looked like, with white hair always tied in either a ponytail or a chignon; I remember that the cookies were always in the shape of a rhombus. Whether eating at home or at a restaurant, what matters to me in a dish is whether it takes me somewhere with my imagination. These cookies did, at the very first bite, so I knew their recipe was worth sharing. Hopefully, it will take you somewhere beautiful as well.

Preparation: 10 minutes
Cooking time: 10 minutes
Passive time: 10 minutes

150 gr. (5.3 oz.) all-purpose flour (or white flour)
100 gr. (3.5 oz.) potato starch
50 gr. (1.8 oz.) unsweetened shredded coconut
2 lemons, juice of one and zest of 2
80 gr. (2.8 oz.) granulated sugar
2.8 fl. oz. (80 ml.) sunflower or almond oil
2 eggs
1 pinch of salt
¼ tsp. of baking powder
1 tsp. vanilla extract or paste

You can also add 30 gr. (2-3 tbsp.) of semi-sweet chocolate chips or white chocolate chips.

Mix the dry ingredients in a mixing bowl.
Add the wet ingredients and mix.

Form 10 patties and press them with a fork to create a pattern and flatten them a little, just like you would do with a burger

Bake for 10-15 minutes at 425°F with convection on.

---

7 *Piazza del Popolo is the main square in town, halfway between the old historic downtown and the train station. The square is paved with a beautiful mosaic that represents the symbol of the town, bees. There are a few stores that surround the square, but they all have changed since I moved. What stayed the same however, is where the market vendors set up their tent every Thursday, including the fish market under the old arcades.*

EARL GREY AND ALMOND COOKIES

FOR 10 COOKIES

These are my favorite cookies. I love earl grey everything, and what happened with these is the perfect balance between the bitterness of the tea, the tangy of the bergamot, and buttery sweetness of the almonds. The Earl Grey scent is subtle and yet long-lasting. After each bite you look for it, you long for it, and so you have another bite. It reminds me of being in London with the band in the summer of 2017; we were staying at the beautiful Corinthia Hotel, and it was when I had my first high tea, with our friends Tony and Christy. I was pregnant with Catherine, and life was about to change forever, on every front. There is something about that experience of London that will stay with me forever, and that will have forever changed me. So, I guess this is a bittersweet cookie, just like earl grey.

Preparation: 10 minutes
Cooking time: 10 minutes
Passive time: 40 minutes (to steep the teabags)

150 gr. (5.3 oz.) almond flour
100 gr. (3.5 oz.) all-purpose flour
100 ml. (3.5 fl. oz.) almond milk
2 teabags of your favorite earl grey tea (*You can also use only loose-leaf,
          and how much depends on how strong you want the flavor.*)
3 tbsp. of your favorite earl grey loose-leaf tea
          (*I have used Fortnum & Mason Countess Grey, my favorite*)
70 gr. (2.5 oz.) sugar
2 candied orange peels (chopped) or just simple orange peels finely chopped,
          even if not candied
2.8 fl. oz. (80 ml.) almond oil
1 tbsp. dark honey (to sweeten the tea)
3 tbsp. (50 gr.) corn starch or potato starch
1 pinch of salt
¼ tsp. baking powder

Before you start working on the dough, prepare the almond latte by steeping 2 teabags and 1 tbsp. of loose-leaf tea in warm almond milk; add the honey, stir, and allow to cool down. Let steep for 15-20 minutes.

Strain the tea and squeeze the teabags (never do this when you are drinking tea, but here I want to get all the bitterness and the tea flavor in the cookies). Set aside.

Mix all the dry ingredients in a mixing bowl, add the loose-leaf tea by roughly breaking them with your hands into the flours.

Finely chop the candied orange and add it to the dough.

Add the oil and the almond milk tea latte and the vanilla extract.

Form 10 patties and bake for 10-12 minutes at 425°F.

These cookies are better enjoyed after a couple of hours.

BLOOD ORANGE AND ROSEMARY CORNMEAL COOKIES

FOR 10 COOKIES

These were some of my most successful quarantine cookies. When I took them to my friend Lydia, the daughter of a pastry chef from Naples, she asked me if she could buy a batch. And that's when I began to realize I was onto something that made me very proud, and happy. Even though they are vegan, they are extremely buttery and crumbly like shortbread. The rosemary gives them a rustic, savory elegance that I love in a dessert. If these cookies were a building, they would be a warm mountain chalet, and the addition of the blood orange juice as a binder gives them a deep, penetrating, and unforgettable essence.

Preparation: 10 minutes
Cooking time: 10 minutes
Passive time: 10 minutes

180 gr. (6.3 oz.) all-purpose flour
120 gr. (4.2 oz.) cornmeal
75 gr. (2.6 oz.) sugar
¼ tsp. vanilla baking powder
1 generous pinch of salt
85 ml. (2.9 fl. oz.) sunflower oil
1 medium sprig of fresh rosemary
Zest of 3 blood oranges
40 ml. (1.3 fl. oz.) freshly squeezed blood orange juice
1½ tbsp. (25 ml.) unsweetened vanilla almond milk

Mix all the dry ingredients, including the finely chopped rosemary and the orange zest.

Add the oil and the juice, then mix.

The dough should be crumbly and only stick together when pressed into a patty.

Form 10 patties, then press them with a fork to give them a nice and rustic look.

Bake for 10-12 minutes at 425°F with convection on.

If you want them sweeter, dust them with powdered sugar after they have cooled down.

PASTE DI MELIGA WITHOUT BUTTER (LEMON CORN COOKIES)

FOR 10 COOKIES

Paste di meliga are a traditional cookie from Piemonte. Meliga, in fact, is an ancient corn flour from the region, which in dialect is called *melia*, or *meira*, from which these cookies take their name. The ingredients are simple: corn flour, butter, sugar, vanilla, and lemon zest. This version, a little softer and without butter, is a little lighter. It can be vegan when replacing buttermilk with almond milk, and because of the addition of lemon juice, it's tarter and lemony.

Preparation: 10 minutes
Cooking time: 10 minutes
Passive time: 10 minutes

180 gr. (6.3 oz.) all-purpose flour
120 gr. (4.2 oz.) cornmeal
75 gr. (2.6 oz.) sugar
¼ tsp. vanilla baking powder
1 generous pinch of salt
85 ml. (2.9 fl. oz.) sunflower oil
½ tsp. vanilla extract
Zest of 1 big lemon (or 2 small ones)
1 tbsp. (10 ml.) freshly squeezed lime juice
2 ½ tbsp. (35 ml.) buttermilk
  (*or unsweetened almond milk if going for a vegan version*)

Mix all the dry ingredients, including the lemon zest.

Add the oil, the buttermilk, and the juice, then mix.

The dough should be crumbly and only stick together when pressed into a patty.

Form ten patties, then press them with a fork to give them a nice and rustic look.

Bake for 10-12 minutes at 425°F.

If you want them sweeter, dust them with powdered sugar after they have cooled down.

CARDAMOM AND MANDARIN SHORTBREAD COOKIES

FOR 10 COOKIES

These simple shortbread cookies are fragrant, intense, magical. It's important to use fresh cardamom pods. They are very quick to make, and they are perfect for an afternoon tea, or for a light dessert after dinner. The cardamom pairs beautifully with herbal ginger tea, black tea, or a classic spiced tea.

Preparation: 15 minutes
Cooking time: 15 minutes
Passive time: 30 minutes to rest the dough

140 gr. (4.9 oz.) salted butter
55 gr. (1.9 oz. or 3½ tbsp.) powdered sugar
185 gr. (6.6 oz.) all-purpose flour
2 mandarins (zest only)
¼ tsp. of fresh cardamom (from pods)
½ tsp. vanilla paste

Remove the cardamom seeds from the pods and grind them to a fine powder with pestle and mortar.

Cream the room-temperature butter in a mixer with the paddle attachment and then add the powdered sugar and the cardamom powder.

Scrape bowl down and add flour and mandarin zest; mix until combined and scrape down the bowl again when needed.

Transfer the dough to a lightly floured surface and roll the dough into a disk. You can also shape the dough into a more traditional rectangle to then create traditional shortbread cookies.
Wrap the dough in plastic film and refrigerate for at least 1 hour.

Pre-heat oven to 350°F, then roll the dough to a little less than ¼-inch thickness. I like these cookies quite thin, even if they tend to create some air bubbles when you bake them. Use your favorite cookie cutter to make the cookies and roll the dough again until you have used it all. If the dough warms up too much, place it in the fridge for a few minutes before rolling it over again to form more cookies. If you have gone for the rectangular shape, cut ½-inch cookies.

Puncture the cookies with a fork, then bake for 10-15 minutes. (I like mine well cooked and slightly browned along the edges).

Allow cookies to completely cool down on a rack before serving.

If you can't find mandarins, you can make these cookies with orange zest. I have used both and they come out sublime no matter what.

SWEET TARALLI WITH RED WINE, ORANGE, AND CARAMELIZED FENNEL SEED

FOR 24 TARALLI

These taralli are the essence of southern Italy. When you eat one, you can see the red soil of Spinazzola, the small town in Puglia where my paternal grandmother Maddalena is from; you can smell the fennel seed, feel the heat of the long summers, hear the crickets, and see Ciccillo, her brother, wearing a white tank, sitting by the window in the late afternoon, where the breeze is drying up the sweat off his forehead. I am very proud of this recipe; it was rewarding to create it, and it thawed memories I believed were frozen forever.

100 ml. (3.4 fl. oz.) red wine
100 ml. (3.4 fl. oz.) almond oil
250 gr. (8.8 oz.) all-purpose flour
1½ tbsp. (20 gr.) honey
Zest of 1 orange
1 pinch of salt
1 tsp. (5 gr.) vanilla baking powder (or regular baking powder)
2 tbsp. sesame seeds
¼ tsp. fennel seed
½ tsp. poppy seeds
½ tsp. vanilla extract
1 cup of white sugar for dipping

In a small non-stick skillet, lightly toast the seeds with a pinch of brown sugar (approximately 5 minutes); a good indication your seeds are well toasted and not burned is the pleasant smell. Remove from the skillet, set aside, and let cool down.

In a mixing bowl, mix red wine, almond oil, vanilla extract, honey, and orange zest.
Add the flour, the baking powder, the salt, and the sesame seeds that will have, by now, cooled down. Start mixing by hand, until the dough is not sticky anymore.

Transfer the dough onto a lightly floured surface and continue mixing until you can form a smooth ball.

Now, take a small piece of dough and roll it out into a 3 ½ or 4-inch rope, join the ends together and gently dip in granulated sugar.

Transfer to baking sheet and continue until you have rolled out all the dough.

Bake for 35-40 minutes at 350°F, using convection for the last five minutes.

They are ready when the bottom is golden brown, and when you can smell the aroma around the house.

Cool down completely on a rack and safe travels to Puglia!

GIANDUIOTTO COOKIES

FOR 10 COOKIES

My home region of Piemonte is famous for its hazelnuts and the combination of hazelnut with chocolate, *gianduja*.

Gianduja, is also a mask in the *commedia dell'arte* that represents the archetypal Piedmontese. These cookies have the basic ingredients of the famous chocolate, and they remind me of home.

Torino was the first capital of Italy (from 1861 to 1865), and it is famous for its elegance, for its cafés, and for its royal, at times austere, beauty. For years, I believe, the city has been underestimated, and it was mostly known for FIAT and Juventus, the soccer team, but after the Winter Olympics of 2006, the world has finally been able to see its beauty, art, and culinary tradition.

And nothing screams Piedmont tradition more than a *gianduiotto*.

Preparation: 10 minutes
Cooking time: 10 minutes
Passive time: 10 minutes

100 gr. (3.5 oz.) all-purpose flour
150 gr. (5.3 oz.) hazelnut meal
2 tbsp. (30 gr.) potato starch
2 tbsp. (30 gr.) baking, raw cocoa powder (unsweetened)
70 gr. (2.5 oz.) of sugar
> (*I like these not too sweet, but you can amp up the sweetness with powdered sugar after they have cooled down, or simply add a little more in the dough.*)

75 ml. (2.5 fl. oz.) hazelnut oil
60 ml. (2 fl. oz. or 4 tbsp.) buttermilk (*you may have to add a little more or use a little less according to the type of flour you use. What you want, is a crumbly dough that sticks together only when pressed into a patty.*)

1 pinch of salt
¼ tsp. baking powder
¼ tsp. vanilla extract
1½ or 2 tbsp. (15 gr.) cup of semi-sweet chocolate chips
2 tbsp. chopped hazelnuts

In a mixing bowl, mix all the dry ingredients.

Add the oil and the buttermilk.

Form 10 patties.

Bake for 10 minutes at 425°F; don't overbake these because you will want a brownie-like consistency, so almost a little undercooked.

PEANUT BUTTER AND JELLY COOKIES

FOR 10 COOKIES

Some food combinations are loved for a reason, and one of the most iconic American ones is peanut butter and jelly. Sometimes I dream about sharing all my creations with my grandmother; I wish she was still alive to see how much she has influenced me, and how much her cooking has made this book and my work possible. She never tried peanut butter.

I became an American citizen on December 19 of 2020, and these cookies are my way of bringing America and Italy together.

Preparation: 15 minutes
Cooking time: 10 minutes
Passive time: 10 minutes

250 gr. (8.8 oz.) all-purpose flour
80 gr. (2.8 oz.) brown sugar
90 ml. (3 fl. oz.) sunflower oil
1 generous pinch of salt
¼ tsp. vanilla extract
¼ tsp. baking powder
60 gr. (2 oz. or 4 tbsp.) of chopped roasted unsalted peanuts
40 gr. (1.5 oz. or 3 tbsp.) dried cranberries
4½ tbsp. (65 ml. or 2.2 fl. oz.) buttermilk or almond milk

In a mixing bowl, mix all the dry ingredients together.

Coarsely chop the peanuts and the cranberries, then add to the mix.

Fold in the wet ingredients. Do not over mix.

Form 10 patties and bake on a baking sheet lined with silicon for 10-12 minutes at 425°F with convection on.

You can add more peanuts and cranberries to taste. Allow to cool down and enjoy!

APPLE PIE IN A COOKIE

FOR 12–13 COOKIES

What's more American than apple pie? Ben's favorite pie is apple pie, but I never made a real one, so one day I surprised him with these: here are my cookies in their apple pie costume. I like to use apples that are not too sweet, like Granny Smith or Pippin, but you can also mix different varieties.

Preparation: 15 minutes
Cooking time: 10-12 minutes
Passive time: 10 minutes

160 gr. (5.6 oz.) almond flour
160 gr. (5.6 oz.) all-purpose flour
75 gr. (2.6 oz. or 5 tbsp.)of sugar
6 tbsp. (85 ml. or 2.9 fl. oz.) of hazelnut oil (*or your favorite vegetable oil*)
1 medium Granny Smith apple, peeled, and chopped bite-sized
¼ tsp. vanilla extract
¼ tsp. baking powder
1 orange (zest)
2 eggs
⅓ cup chopped pecans
Cardamom, cinnamon, ginger, cloves, and nutmeg to taste
   (*the trick here is always to taste the dough and follow your instinct.*)

Pre-heat oven to 425°F.

In a mixing bowl, mix all dry ingredients, then add the apple and the pecans. When it comes to spices, go with your taste, and pick the ones you like the most. Instead of measuring spoons, start by sprinkling them into the mix and smell the dough; after adding the wet ingredients you'll be able to taste and decide whether to add more spices or not.

Now add the wet ingredients and mix well. Do not over-mix.

With the help of a spoon, form small patties, and with a fork flatten them on the baking sheet that you have previously lined with parchment paper. I like to give these cookies a rustic look, a non-perfect one, a warm, homey feel that an apple pie never fails to deliver.

Bake for 10 minutes and allow to cool.

ICONIC RECIPES
FROM INSTAGRAM

◎ @ALICECARBONETENCH

Instagram to Table

NOTE

I don't have a favorite recipe. Yet, if I had to choose a handful with a special place in my heart, it would be those that follow in this chapter. It's not that they're tastier or healthier than the others in this book. It's because they were part of some of the most beautiful episodes of Instagram to Table and of my Instagram feed, where we all gather every day as if it were our communal kitchen table.

When I look back at how my online show started with a simple bruschetta, when I was still living in Tarzana, I can't help but feel not only pride, but also deep gratitude for each friend who religiously followed me—week after week.

When I say that food heals me, I should always mention that it is the sharing of the food that helped me most—sharing it in person, of course, but equally on Instagram, on my website, show after show. You who witnessed are part of my healing. You inspired me every week to create something new, something delicious, something different. I healed with food, but I also healed with you.

Do you remember when my friend Zoey came over for lavender and honey cassata, or when Erica did, and baked with me tangerine coconut cookies? With my friend Kate we made flatbread, and we even had Los Angeles councilwoman Nithya Raman during her election campaign. My friend Sofia talked about sourdough, and some of you joined the show from your kitchens. With Benmont always present, my rock, we tried it all. "Hi guys" became our signature dish, and "I love you, guys" was a truth, not just four words used without intention.

I am a lucky girl to have had you all by my side. I shared with you Christmas of 2020, a difficult one because of the pandemic, as well as my 39th birthday. I shared with you all my joys, my achievements, my fears, my pain, and you did the same. These are the ingredients that ultimately made this book, and this section is a dedication to the very beginning, to how it started, so that we can keep going on without forgetting that together we went very far.

STINGING NETTLE RISOTTO

FOR 4 PEOPLE

This recipe is very dear to me because it is one of those dishes that reminds me of my childhood, of a time when things were simple, of a time when the air was cleaner and wild asparagus grew with stinging nettles by the side of the street, and you could simply give them a quick rinse without worrying too much about the smog and dirt on them. My grandmother picked stinging nettles every spring, often right outside of her house, along the road that connected her house to the elementary school my brother and I attended. I have a very vivid memory of it.

She would also pick a type of vegetable called *luvertin*, something I haven't eaten since she passed. *Luvertin*, or *luppolo selvatico* (wild hop), makes a great addition to this risotto, if you can find it, as well as a beautiful spring frittata.

Stinging nettles aren't easy to find; at the Hollywood Farmers Market, where I go every Sunday, there is only one vendor that has it, for a short time, every spring.

I will never forget how I felt the first time I made stinging nettles for Ben and Catherine, when we moved to Los Angeles (close to the market) from Tarzana. I had not had stinging nettles since the death of my grandmother (picking and cleaning them takes long), and it's one of those traditions that not many young people have the patience and the time to pass on and keep alive.

I will never forget how I felt when I made them for Ben and Catherine because I cried. I cried tears of joy.

With stinging nettles, you can also make a beautiful spring soup with rice and potatoes (very similar to the spinach and potato one in this book).

Preparation: 1 hour
Cooking time: 20-25 minutes

500 gr. (17 oz.) of stinging nettles (weight is after the stems have been removed)
320 gr. (11.3 oz. or approximately 1 ¼ cup) of arborio rice
1 shallot
3-4 cups of vegetable broth (or water)
Butter and extra-virgin olive oil to taste
A generous splash of white wine for deglazing
Salt to taste
Parmigiano to taste

Without touching them, throw the stinging nettles in salted boiling water, stems and all, and cook 3-4 minutes.

When they have boiled for a bit, drain them and place them in a big pasta colander on a bed of ice.

Remove the leaves from the stem. You can do this without gloves because they don't sting anymore. It is a bit of a messy job, but trust me, you'll be thankful in the end.

Throw away the stems and, with an immersion blender, purée the leaves.

Now proceed like you would do for any risotto: finely chop the shallot in a mix of butter and extra-virgin olive oil until golden, then add the rice and toast it for a few minutes, until it becomes translucent. Add the white wine and cook until evaporated.

Add enough broth to cover the rice and cook for 5 minutes. Stinging nettles beautifully pair with asparagus, so when you make the vegetable broth, if you can, add some asparagus ends or frozen asparagus to enhance the flavor of the nettles.

Now add the stinging nettle cream to the rice, stir, and keep cooking adding broth whenever necessary, whenever the rice starts to dry up.

When the rice is cooked through (approximately 15-20 minutes), turn off the heat, add a little bit of butter, and stir.[8]

Serve immediately with grated parmigiano to taste.

---

8 In Italian, this process is called "mantecatura." There is no real translation for it, even though it is a fundamental part of risotto-making. It is basically the act of incorporating cold butter into the hot risotto off the heat and when the cooking has completed to create a creamy rice.

PIZZETTE AND SALATINI (ITALIAN APERITIF)

FOR 8–10 PEOPLE

We made this fun recipe during one of the first episodes of Instagram to Table, from the Tarzana house. I remember the phone being on the counter and not held by the more-fancy ring light I purchased in the new house. I remember the production being much less sophisticated than it became with time, but I remember the same deep, fun, and real conversations we had.

This is a traditional Italian aperitif, often enjoyed with olives, good cheese, a glass of wine, a Campari or, for those who don't drink, a classic Crodino[9] my favorite alcohol-free aperitif drink. Pizzettas are, of course, small pizzas made of puff pastry, while *salatini*, which can be filled with your favorite vegetables or protein, are spirals or puff pastry bites filled with spinach, cheese, artichokes, or tuna, or bell peppers.

Note: My favorite filling is bell pepper and anchovies but being the only one in the family who eats bell peppers, I always end up using what Catherine and Ben love. If using bell peppers, cut them in thin slivers with a mandolin, and substitute for the spinach, also adding anchovy fillets. You can fill these with canned tuna and bell peppers, with sautéed artichokes, with sausages, with cheese, with ham, or with asparagus.

Preparation: 25 minutes
Cooking time: 15-20 minutes

12 sheets of store-bought puff pastry
1 cup of tomato sauce
1 cup of black olives (pitted)
½ cup capers
200 gr. (7 oz.) of spinach (*or your favorite green*)
1 egg
2 tbsp. milk or buttermilk
Extra-virgin olive oil, salt, and pepper to taste

Pre-heat oven to 400°F.

Slice the olives horizontally to form small rings.

For the pizzettas, take the puff pastry out of the freezer 20 minutes before making these. On a lightly floured surface, roll out the puff pastry to make it slightly larger than the rectangle it comes in, then cut out 2½ inch circles with a cookie cutter or a glass.

Transfer the pizzettas to a baking sheet lined with parchment paper, puncture them with a fork, and brush them with the egg wash.

Top them all with some tomato sauce, a few capers, and a few pieces of olives. You can also add anchovies if you'd like.

9 *Crodino is an Italian sparkling bitter soda served as an alcohol-free option during aperitif.*

Sprinkle some dry oregano, and salt, and bake until golden, approximately 15 minutes.

For the *salatini*:

Rinse the spinach and sauté it in a little bit of butter or olive oil, salt to taste, add a pinch of sugar and when cooked, blend it into a smooth cream with an immersion blender. Set aside and allow to cool completely.

Just like we did with the pizzettas, take the puff pastry out of the freezer 20 minutes before rolling it out.

On a lightly floured surface, roll out the puff pastry and create 1½ to 2-inch strips. Transfer to the baking sheet lined with parchment paper, puncture them with a fork, brush them all with egg wash and add a small amount of spinach cream.

Now roll the strips to form little cones or your desired shape that can hold the filling and brush the outer surface with the egg wash.

Bake until golden, approximately 15 minutes.

LEMON CRACKERS

FOR APPROXIMATELY 30 CRACKERS

These crackers are our daily breakfast. I make them with lemon or orange zest, or with herbs de Provence, with sesame seeds, fennel seeds, or poppy seeds. This is to say, once you master the basic recipe, you can make your own and have fun with the most creative flavor combinations. And you will never buy crackers again.

Preparation: 30 minutes
Cooking time: 15 minutes

150 gr. (5.3 oz.) white flour
100 gr. (3.5 oz.) durum wheat flour
7 tsp. (35 ml.) extra-virgin olive oil
Your favorite flavor (*or simply sea salt*)
Zest of 1 lemon (*or your favorite flavoring*)
1½ tsp. (15-20 ml.) white wine
95-100 ml. (3.2-3.3 fl. oz.) water
2½ tsp. (10 gr.) sea salt

Mix all the ingredients in a mixing bowl until you form a soft, easy-to-handle dough that doesn't stick. This is a very easy dough to make, and you will learn it takes only a few minutes to reach the desired consistency.

Knead the dough for a few minutes and then wrap it in plastic film; allow to rest for 15 minutes or overnight, in the fridge.

Roll out small portions of dough at a time and form very thin rectangles, which will then become your crackers. I make this dough every other day and I don't have the time to create perfectly shaped crackers. So, what I do, is bake big rectangles and then I break them into smaller crackers once they have baked and cooled down.

Bake at 400°F for 15-20 minutes or until golden.

Cool down and keep in an airtight container for up to 3 days.

Note: you can dust these with powdered sugar and have a lovely semi-sweet cracker. You can also chop 1 tablespoon of Buddha's hand in the dough, and you will have created one of the most sublime flavor combinations. We eat these crackers for breakfast with some honey, and I even dip them in my coffee.

SEMI-SWEET CHOCOLATE CRACKERS

FOR 35–40 CRACKERS

These crackers are an adaptation from the lemon crackers, and they are my go-to for a dessert without too much sugar. You can also make them plain by substituting coconut flour or simply more white flour for the cocoa powder. If you make them plain, I'd add 10 more gr. of sugar, and more vanilla paste.

Preparation: 30 minutes
Cooking time: 10-12 minutes

230 gr. (8.1 oz. or approximately 1¾ cup) of all-purpose flour
1½ tbsp. (20 gr.) of unsweetened cocoa powder
45 ml. (1.5 oz. or approximately ¼ cup) of sunflower or almond oil
Zest of 2 oranges (optional)
1 generous pinch of salt
4 tbsp. (50 gr.) of brown sugar
½ tbsp. vanilla paste
100 ml. (3.4 fl. oz.) of room-temperature filtered water
A touch of cinnamon (optional)
¼ tsp. almond extract (optional)

Mix all the ingredients in a mixing bowl until you form a soft, easy-to-handle dough that doesn't stick. Like for regular crackers, the dough is easy to make, and you will learn it takes only a few minutes to reach the desired consistency, with either method.

Knead the dough for a few minutes and then wrap in plastic film; allow to rest for 15 minutes or overnight, in the fridge.

Roll out small portions of dough at a time and form very thin rectangles, which will then become your crackers.

Bake at 400°F for 10-15 minutes, but check after 10 minutes, because with cocoa it can be difficult to see when they are ready; they tend to burn very easily.

When the crackers have cooled down completely, dust them with powdered sugar. Wait at least 1 hour before eating them, as the flavor needs that long to fully develop.

Note: the first time I made these, when I was experimenting for the book, I didn't like them right out of the oven. When I ate them two hours later, the flavor had completely changed, and they are now some of our favorite semi-cookies to have as dessert after dinner.

PASSION FRUIT AND CITRUS JELLY WITH WHIPPED CREAM AND PISTACHIOS

FOR 4 SERVINGS

We made this jelly on the show to pair with vegan brownies.

After the show, because Catherine loves this jelly so much, I started playing with adding grapefruit and any citrus I had at home. I like to sweeten it simply with honey, and this healthy recipe becomes a fun and delicious way to get your vitamin C in. For a more decadent dessert, I pair it with a simple whipped cream sweetened with a touch of maple syrup and infused with vanilla.

I prepare this in a 6x4 (or similar) rectangular container with a lid and cut it into squares or rectangles that I then top with the cream.

Preparation: 10 minutes
Passive time: at least 6 hours for cooling down and solidifying

6-7 passion fruit (seeds removed). The total amount of juice should be a little over a cup for a perfect juice/gelatin ration.
1 grapefruit
1 small orange or tangerine
1 bag of gelatin
1½ tsp. honey (or to taste)
1 cup of heavy cream (cold)
1 tsp. vanilla paste (to split between the whipping cream and the jelly)
½ cup unsalted pistachios
Maple syrup for the whipping cream, to taste

Pass the passion fruit pulp through a strainer to remove the seeds and get as much juice as possible. I have found that if I heat up the pulp in the microwave for just a few seconds, it makes it easier to separate the juice from seeds. Pour the juice into a small saucepan and add the squeezed juice of the grapefruit.

Squeeze the orange in the container you will use for jelly and sprinkle the gelatin powder over it.

Bring the passion fruit and the grapefruit to a simmer, then remove from the heat and sweeten it with the honey and a touch of vanilla paste.

Add the warm juice to the cold orange juice.

Mix it very well until the gelatin is completely dissolved (5 minutes).
Cover with the lid and place in the fridge until it turns into jelly.

Whip the cream.

Fill a pastry bag with a decorative nozzle and set aside.

When the jelly is ready, you can either enjoy as is (Catherine loves to eat little squares of wobbly orange jelly) or cut into rectangular wedges, transfer to a small dessert plate, and top with little roses of whipped cream. Finish with chopped pistachios, roasted and unsalted.

RICOTTA AND LAVENDER CASSATA WITH CHEDDAR CHEESE

FOR 4 JARS

I made this beautiful dessert on the New Year's Eve episode of Instagram to Table. It is, to this day, one of my favorites; it was shot by my friend Zoey Taylor. This dessert is a marvel, the perfect combination of sweet and savory, perfect for those, like me, who tend to prefer a good cheese board with honey to a tiramisu for dessert. The key is in the quality of the cheese and of the ricotta, as well as in the trust you put in your taste. Lavender, in fact, can be tricky if misused. Keep tasting your cream and follow your instinct. When you think it's right it means it is. This is a playful take on one of my favorite Sicilian desserts, *cassata siciliana*, traditionally made with sheep ricotta, almond paste, and candied citrus. I am using almond-based cookies instead of sponge to have the "marzipan" effect.

Preparation: 45 minutes
Cooking time: 15 minutes
Passive time: 1-2 hours to drain the ricotta

400 gr. (14 oz. or approximately 1½ cup) of sheep ricotta (*When I can't find sheep ricotta, I add ¼ cup of plain goat cheese (or to taste) to a regular cow's ricotta to give it the sheep flavor that is characteristic of Italian cassata. If you don't like sheep milk, however, you can make this dessert with plain cow's milk ricotta or even with vegan almond ricotta.*)
2 lavender cookies
50 gr. (1.7 oz.) of sharp cheddar cheese
3 tbsp. lavender honey, or a mix of dark honey and lavender syrup
Lavender syrup to taste (optional)
1 tsp. edible lavender flowers
1 small sprig of rosemary
Vanilla extract to taste
½ cup candied orange peel or to taste (recipe follows next)

For 17 lavender cookies:

100 gr. (3.5 oz.) of all-purpose flour
150 gr. (5.3 oz.) of almond flour
1 big lemon (zest) or 2 small
1 tsp. vanilla paste
¼ cup (40 ml.) of buttermilk or almond milk
2.5 fl. oz. (75 ml.) of almond oil
2-3 drops of almond extract
75 gr. (2.6 oz.) of caster sugar or light brown cane sugar
1 tsp. edible lavender flowers
1 generous pinch of salt
1 pinch of baking powder

Drain the ricotta through a colander to get rid of all the water. I usually let it drain for a couple of hours before making this dessert.

Make the cookies like the usual cookies we have made in the "Cookies" section. Mix the dry ingredients, grind the lavender flower to a powder, zest the lemon, and then add the wet ingredients. Do not overmix. Form 17 balls, arrange them on a baking sheet lined with parchment paper, and lightly press them down with a fork. (Remember, we are going to crumble these, but those that are left will be a perfect treat for any dessert or afternoon tea).

Bake the cookies at 425°F for 15 minutes. Allow the cookies to completely cool down on a rack.

While the cookies bake, in a mixing bowl, whip the ricotta with the honey and with the goat cheese (if you haven't found sheep ricotta).

Finely slice the cheddar using a mandolin and set it aside.

Chop the candied orange zest bitesize and add them to the ricotta cream.

Finely chop the lavender flowers and the rosemary and add to the ricotta cream. If you want, you can also add some lavender syrup here, perhaps reducing the amount of honey. But go with your taste.

Choose 4 pretty jars and let's start layering the trifles.

Spread a small amount of ricotta cream on the bottom of the jar and then crumble some cookies. Add a few slices of cheddar cheese and start again with cream, crumbled cookies, and cheese until the very top.

Finish the last layer with a thin slice of cheddar cheese and, when ready to serve, drizzle some honey on top.

If prepared in advance, keep the dessert refrigerated, and only drizzle the honey right before serving. This dessert keeps in the fridge for 3 days, covering the top of each jar.

CHOCOLATE-COVERED CANDIED ORANGE PEELS INFUSED WITH CINNAMON

FOR 25–30 TREATS

This is one of my father's favorite sweet treats. The combination of orange and chocolate is a classic for a reason: because it is good.

In Italy, you find these beautiful orange treats in the best pastry shops, *pasticcerie*, and now you can make them at home for a daily indulgence that is also a way to reduce waste and use all the orange peels you would otherwise throw away. It's important to use organic oranges and good quality chocolate.

Preparation time: 15 minutes + 1-2 hours rest
Cooking time: 15 minutes + 20 for the chocolate

200 gr. (7 oz.) of orange peels (approximately 4 big oranges),
organic and weighed after soaking.
200 gr. (7 oz.) of brown sugar
200 ml. (6.7 fl. oz.) of water
150 gr. (5.3 oz.) of dark chocolate
1 stick of cinnamon

For this recipe you need a chocolate thermometer if you decide to temper the chocolate.

Peel the oranges and cut the peel lengthwise, into ¼-inch strips.

Soak the peels in cold water for 1-2 hours.

Delicately remove any excess pith with a small knife, then weigh the peels after they have soaked, and discharge the water.

In a medium saucepan, mix an equal amount of water and sugar. Add orange peels. (Water, sugar, and oranges should have the same weight.)

Add the stick of cinnamon and bring to a boil.

Lower the heat and cook until the water has been absorbed and a smooth syrup begins to form. This takes approximately 15 minutes. I never let the syrup thicken too much because it makes the peels difficult to handle, and there is a risk of crystallization. You want the orange peels to be shiny.

After 15 minutes, remove the peels (be very careful, because the syrup is very hot) and delicately transfer them to a baking sheet lined with parchment paper or silicon, or to a big plate, orange side up, to cool down completely. Do not use paper towel.

Ideally, you will want to temper your chocolate before dipping the orange peels. But if you don't have the time, you can melt the chocolate in a double boiler, and when melted, dip one-half of the orange peels. Place them to cool down completely on the same parchment paper.

If you want to temper the chocolate and have a shinier look, melt 2/3 of the chocolate in a double boiler, stirring often, until the thermometer registers around 115°F. Do not get higher than 120°F and make sure the chocolate doesn't touch the water.

Remove from the double boiler and gradually add in the remaining chocolate to bring the temperature down, stirring vigorously and constantly, until the temperature drops to 84°F (10-15 minutes).

Reheat the chocolate briefly by placing the bowl back over the double boiler until it reaches 89°F, and making sure it doesn't get higher than 91°F. Do not leave the chocolate on the double boiler when dipping the orange peels, place it back on it from time to time if the temperature drops; 89°F is considered "working temperature."

I know it sounds complicated, but after you practice a few times, I promise you it isn't. Tempering the chocolate is extremely rewarding when eating it, and feeling it snap under your teeth before finding the softness of the orange.

STUFFED PEACHES WITH AMARETTI AND CHOCOLATE

FOR 6 PEOPLE

This recipe is another classic dessert from Piemonte, also one of my all-time summer favorites. It's a dessert that is decadent without being heavy, and it truly holds the magical scents of summer.

Preparation: 15 minutes
Cooking time: 25-30 minutes (according to how big the nectarines are)

6 big ripe yellow peaches (nectarines can also be used)
1½ tbsp. (20 gr.) of raw, unsweetened cocoa
150 gr. (5.3 oz. or approximately ¾ cup) of crunchy amaretti cookies, like Lazzaroni
40 gr. (1.4 oz.) of dark chocolate, 75% and up
Vanilla and almond extract to taste
½ tbsp. of brown sugar (or to taste)

Cut the peach in half, remove the pit, and carefully scoop out some of the pulp, so that the peach can hold the filling. Set aside the pulp and save every bit of juice; this will make the filling soft and very flavorful.

Shave the chocolate and break the amaretti cookies in a mixing bowl. Add the extracts and the sugar.

Finely chop the peach pulp and add to the amaretti and the chocolate. Mix the filling with a spoon.

Stuff the peaches with the filling and bake for 30 minutes at 400°F.

Allow to cool down and enjoy either as they are or with a scoop of vanilla gelato.

This dessert keeps for 2-3 days in the fridge.

ASPARAGUS SALAD WITH ROASTED FENNEL AND NAVY BEANS

FOR 2 PEOPLE

This is one of those dishes that is a go-to during a busy week, but when I still want to eat a good lunch, possibly at the table and not on the run. I love the pairing of fennel and asparagus, and I love that the only cooking required, in the oven, allows me to be in another room and not at the stove.

Preparation: 15 minutes
Cooking time: 15 minutes

1 can of navy beans
1 bunch fresh asparagus
1 fennel
1 leek
Salt, pepper, and extra-virgin olive oil to taste
Zest and juice of ½ a lemon (or to taste)

Wash the vegetables, leave the asparagus whole but thinly slice the fennel and the leek. (I use the mandolin for the leek, but the knife for the fennel because I like it thicker.) Remove the tops and the bottom of the fennel and save the discard for stock.

Arrange the vegetables on a baking sheet and drizzle with some olive oil. Add salt and pepper, give it a mix, and bake at 400°F for 10-15 minutes, perhaps mixing the vegetables in between, after 5 minutes.

While the veggies roast, rinse the canned beans.

When the vegetables are ready, chop the asparagus and, in a salad bowl, mix with the beans and add some fresh dill, if you have it.

Dress the salad with salt flakes, extra-virgin olive oil, black pepper, lemon juice, and some lemon zest to taste.

SOFT FOCACCINAS

FOR 9 FOCACCINAS

These *focaccinas* are something in between a pita and a naan. This is the base, you can top them with anything you want, or simply enjoy them as they are, divine. I have also made them with sourdough starter, and the ingredients are in the notes. We made these when the guest of the show was Nithya Raman, the candidate Ben and I supported for city council to represent district 4 of Los Angeles. She won, and she approved of the naans.

I love to spread a thin layer of honey and eat them warm.

Preparation: 10 minutes
Cooking time: 15 minutes
Passive time: 3-4 hours (until dough has doubled in size)

265 gr. (9.3 oz. or approximately 2 cups) of bread flour
4 tbsp. (50 gr.) of whole milk yogurt
1¼ tsp. (5-7 gr.) of sea salt
150 ml. (5 fl. oz. or approximately ¾ cup) of room-temperature filtered water
1 pinch of brown sugar
1 tsp. (5 gr.) of dry active yeast

Dissolve the dry yeast in the warm water, add a pinch of sugar and let it rest for 5-10 minutes to activate.

Add flour, yogurt, and salt and mix by hand until the dough comes together, is not sticky, but is still soft.

Move the dough onto a lightly floured surface and knead for 5 minutes.

Form a ball and move to a lightly oiled mixing bowl; cover with a plate and place in the oven with the light on, to proof, for 3-4 hours, until the dough has doubled in size. I like to turn the oven on for just a few seconds to create the perfect warm environment for the dough to proof.

On a lightly floured surface, make 7-8 balls and allow to rest for 10 minutes, covered with a damp cloth.

On the stove, warm up a small cast iron pan, lid on, for a good five minutes. A warm pan is key to a perfect naan, and you will see that, if your cast iron isn't hot enough, your second or third naan will be better than the first.

Roll out the first ball, either with your hands or a rolling pin, then put it in the hot cast iron pan, lid on.

Cook for a few minutes on both sides and move on to the rest.

Eat warm.

These are perfect with honey, or some extra-virgin olive oil and salt flakes, as a sandwich instead of bread, with olive tapenade, or with Nutella!

If you are using a sourdough starter, change the ingredients as follows:

8 tbsp. (100 gr.) ripe sourdough starter
200 gr. (7 oz.) flour (less flour to compensate the flour in the starter)
2 fl. oz. (60 ml.) water

The sourdough dough will take approximately 5 hours to proof until doubled.

ORANGE BLOSSOM
LINGUE DI GATTO

This simple wafer-thin cookie is a staple of both French and Italian pastries. It is very easy and quick to make, and the name comes from their elongated shape that resembles (tradition says) the tongue of a cat.

Preparation: 10 minutes
Cooking time: 10 minutes

50 gr. (1.7 oz.) of egg white (approximately 2 eggs)
Approximately 4½ tbsp. (45 gr.) of powdered sugar
5 tbsp., packed (50 gr.) of all-purpose flour
5 tbsp. (50 gr.) of unsalted butter softened at room temperature
1 pinch of salt
A few drops of orange blossom extract
> *(it must be subtle and elegant, and like every extract, orange blossom can quickly become overpowering and taste like perfume.)*

Whisk together the egg whites and the powdered sugar until they form a smooth cream. Add the butter and the extract, then the flour.

Fill a pastry bag with the creamy dough and a flat tip and form 15-20 4-inch-long cookies.

Bake for 10 minutes at 390°F.

Delicately remove from the baking sheet and allow to cool down completely until crunchy.

SOURDOUGH GRANOLA WITH GINGER AND HERBS DE PROVENCE

FOR 4 MEDIUM JARS

I created this dish as a gift to my friend Julianna, when her father Ray passed away of Covid-19 on May 13th, 2020. I loved Julianna's dad; I remember taking him to see his daughter perform a Christmas show with Rufus Wainwright and Carrie Fisher at Royce Hall, UCLA. Julianna is one of my oldest friends in Los Angeles, and I wanted to give her something from my heart, that would warm her heart, so I baked this granola and made jars of love for her.

It also became a great way to use a sourdough starter discard.

This is for you, Ray Pitt.

Preparations: 10 minutes
Cooking time: 40-50 minutes

160 gr. (5.6 oz. or approximately ½ cup) of ripe sourdough starter
250 gr. (8.8 oz. or approximately 3 cups) of Swiss muesli or old-fashioned rolled oats
30 ml. (2 tbsp.) of maple syrup
1 tbsp. honey
1 tsp. sesame seed
1 tsp. chia seeds
1 tsp. coconut flakes (optional)
4 tbsp. (50 gr.) of chopped walnuts or hazelnuts
50-60 ml. (4 tbsp.) of hazelnut oil (*I love the aroma this oil gives the granola, but you can also use walnut oil or almond oil*)
¼ tsp. vanilla extract
1 pinch Himalayan pink salt
1 pinch dry herbs de Provence
Chopped candied ginger, to taste
Chopped candied orange, to taste
Chopped dried apricot, to taste
Zest of 1 small lemon

You can substitute hazelnuts with your favorite nuts: pecans, pistachios, almonds...
You can substitute candied orange and ginger with your favorite dried fruits: cranberries, plums, dates, raisins. If you are using oats instead of Swiss muesli, feel free to add more fruit.

Pre-heat oven to 300°F, possibly with convection on.

Chop the ginger and the nuts (if adding nuts).

In a mixing bowl, mix all the ingredients.

Spread the thick mix onto a baking sheet lined with silicone or parchment paper.

Bake for 35-50 minutes until nicely golden and hard. Check on it after 30 minutes. I cooked mine for close to 40 because I wanted it a little darker, but it's up to your taste (and your oven).

Allow to cool down, then break the granola into clusters.

Dust with powdered sugar, if you want, or add salt flakes, or eat it the way it is. I love to snack on it, but you can add this to your yogurt, milk, soup (if savory), etc.

Note: You can add more sugar, change the seeds, add chopped dry cranberries or raisins (I used muesli, so there were raisins and nuts already), but you can chop a handful of almonds or walnuts, pecans or hazelnuts, dried apricots, chocolate chips...you name it. You can also make a sweet/spicy/savory version and add smoked paprika and chili flakes.

I really love the addition of the rosemary and lavender that are in the herbs de Provence!

TOFU PIZZAIOLA

FOR 4 PEOPLE

I made this unbelievably good tofu on the show in the month of July 2020; I was looking for ways to enjoy and want tofu, rather than endure it. This has pretty much become my mission and philosophy with food: after years of eating nutrients, I want to eat food for the taste of it. So, I always cook everything to be something I crave rather than something I must eat because of whatever vitamin, protein, or good fat they have.

Preparation: 15 minutes
Cooking time: 20 minutes
Passive time: 5 minutes

400 gr. (14 oz.) of extra-firm organic tofu
1 big fresh tomato and a handful of cherry tomatoes, or 250 gr. of tomato sauce
½ yellow onion, finely chopped
1 clove garlic
Fresh and dry oregano (dry is essential and fresh is optional)
Capers and good olives, to taste; I used a lot of both because I wanted the flavor to really come through, so probably a good ¼ cup of capers—chopped and 15-20 *Taggiasca* olives, pitted.
> (*These olives are small but big in flavor, and they are grown primarily in the Alpes-Maritimes region of Liguria, in Italy.*)

Extra-virgin olive oil, salt, pepper, and chili flakes, to taste
Anchovy juice, optional
1 pinch of palm sugar (or brown sugar)

Cut the tofu into 10-15 rectangular slices and set aside.

In a big non-stick skillet, sauté the onion and garlic clove in olive oil, then add the tomatoes, salt, pepper, and a pinch of brown sugar (possibly palm sugar). Remove the garlic.

Finely chop the capers and pit the olives.

Add them to the sauce with the dry and fresh oregano, simmer for 5 minutes, and add the tofu. Cook the tofu at low heat, occasionally stirring and adding water for a good 30-35 minutes. It's important to allow plenty of time for the tofu to absorb all the flavors. I cooked it a low heat for a long time, adding some water when it seemed to be drying up.

Cover the skillet and allow to rest for at least 15 minutes. The steam and the heat really allow all the beautiful pizza flavors to be absorbed by the tofu.

Note: For a full "pizza experience," after the tofu is fully cooked, transfer it to a round pizza dish, top it with fresh mozzarella to taste and bake it for 15 minutes at 400°F.

POLPETTE DI PANE
(BREAD MEATBALLS)

FOR APPROXIMATELY 15 MEATBALLS

My father suggested this recipe almost since the beginning of the Instagram show, in 2019. This simple dish is traditional of Puglia, where he was born, as well as of the poor culinary history of the region. In rough times, when meat wasn't available, bread and eggs were all a meatball could be made of. They are easy to make and delicious to eat. At 99-years-old, my grandmother Maddalena still makes these.

Preparation: 10 minutes
Cooking time 20-40 minutes
(according to the type of cooking and whether you go for tomato sauce or not)

300 gr. (10.5 oz.) of good bread, possibly stale
(*I love ciabatta or baguette*) broken into pieces
4 eggs
Breadcrumbs, as needed
100 gr. (3.5 oz. or approximately 1 cup) of grated Parmigiano cheese
1 small clove of garlic (or to taste)
1 small carrot
½ a zucchini
2 tbsp. chopped parsley (or to taste)
Salt, pepper, and extra-virgin olive oil to taste

Soak the bread in water for 10 minutes, (crust and all).

Remove the heart of the garlic and chop it finely.

Peel the carrot and chop it very finely, finely chop the zucchini as well, and sauté in extra-virgin olive oil for 10 minutes.

In a mixing bowl, grate the parmesan cheese, add the chopped garlic, the parsley, and the eggs. Mix well, add salt and pepper and the sautéed vegetables.

Squeeze all the water out of the bread and add it to the egg mixture, breaking it into pieces with your hands.

Form the meatballs with your hands and cook following your desired method. I like to sauté the meatballs in a little bit of extra virgin olive oil until nice and browned, and then continue cooking them in tomato sauce for 15 minutes.

If you decide to bake them, bake for 15-20 minutes at 400°F.

These meatballs are perfect with pasta or as they are, with the tomato sauce. You can also add green peas, bell peppers, corn, or your favorite vegetables to it.

TEGOLE VALDOSTANE WITH BUTTERMILK AND A PINCH OF TURMERIC

FOR 24 COOKIES

As you have gathered from the stories in this book, I am deeply in love with everything about Valle d'Aosta. These cookies, a traditional recipe from the mountains, are no exception. One day, on the show, I decided to make them to accompany a traditional coffee drink from Piemonte, *Bicerin* (recipe follows), but I didn't have eggs in the fridge. Like I have been doing during the pandemic, I didn't go out just to buy them, as I have been enjoying using up all that I have before a masked trip to the grocery store. So, I created this variation of it without the traditional egg whites and with much less butter. They came out divine, and I have been following my very own recipe ever since.

Preparation: 10 minutes
Cooking time: 15-20 minutes

200 gr. (7 oz.) of hazelnut flour
75 gr. (2.6 oz.) of brown sugar
60 gr. (2.1 oz. or approximately 4½ tbsp.) salted butter
      (if using unsalted butter, add a generous pinch of salt to the dough)
Vanilla extract or paste to taste (optional)
4 tbsp. (60 ml.) of buttermilk
1 pinch of turmeric

Pre-heat the oven to 350°F with convection on.

In a mixing bowl, mix flour, turmeric, sugar, and the butter previously softened at room temperature.

Add the buttermilk. We want a semi-fluid dough, a very creamy one.

On a baking sheet lined with silicone, place a spoonful of dough and then spread it around in a circular shape by delicately tapping with your index finger until you create a 4-inch, very thin circle. Bake for 15 minutes or until nicely browned.

Allow to completely cool down and become crunchy. This is a wafer-thin cookie that is supposed to be crispy.

BICERIN OF TURIN

FOR 2 PEOPLE

This drink is what I made on the show together with the Tegole Valdostane on a summer episode. Bicerin, in the dialect of Piedmont, means "little glass," where traditionally this drink is served.

It is so good that Umberto Eco wrote about it in his novel *The Prague Cemetery*. It has been loved over the centuries by writers, politicians, musicians, and actors, and to this day it is loved by every person who tries it. I like it with unsweetened espresso, but if you like very sweet drinks, you may sweeten your coffee while making it. It's important to choose a quality coffee and a quality chocolate.

> 3½ tbsp. (50 ml.) heavy whipping cream
> ½ tsp. maple syrup
> 100 gr. (3.5 oz.) of dark chocolate (75%)
> 100 ml. (3.4 fl. oz., or approximately ½ cup) of espresso (with stovetop Italian mocha)
> ¼ cup milk (I used almond milk)

Melt the chocolate in a small saucepan or double boiler; when it's melted, add the milk, and stir to create a smooth hot chocolate cream.

Hand-whip the cream with the maple syrup. It doesn't need to be fully whipped, just semi, and slightly thicker.

Make the coffee (I use an old traditional Italian stovetop mocha).

Choose your favorite glass and start composing the drink by pouring the hot chocolate first. If it has firmed while preparing the cream, just heat it up again with a little more milk.

Now pour the coffee over the chocolate, and lastly the semi-whipped cream.
Dust with unsweetened cocoa powder and enjoy hot.

FRESH FAVA BEAN SALAD WITH PECORINO CHEESE

FOR 4 PEOPLE

This is a go-to, during the few weeks of spring when fresh fava beans are available at the market. They remind me of my paternal grandmother, of Puglia, of good things coming.

Preparation: 30 minutes
Cooking time: 15 minutes

3½ pounds of fresh fava beans (weight is with shell on)
½ cup shaved pecorino cheese
Extra-virgin olive oil, lemon juice and black pepper to taste.

Shell the fava beans, then blanch them for 2-3 minutes in salted boiling water.

Drain them and, as soon as they cool down enough to be handled, remove the outer skin, and set aside.

Slice the pecorino cheese very thin, with a mandolin.

In a salad bowl, dress the fava beans with extra-virgin olive oil, salt, pepper, and lemon juice to taste; add the sliced pecorino cheese right before serving.

Note: If this is an appetizer, it can serve 4 people, maybe with some good bread or crostini, and the addition of extra pecorino cheese. To make it more of a complete dish, you can add 1 bunch of grilled asparagus, and 1 thinly sliced raw fennel.

CATHERINE'S FAIRY OATMEAL

FOR 3 PEOPLE

This oatmeal is a staple in our house, especially since Catherine is obsessed with it. In Italy oatmeal is not popular, but it's one of those breakfast dishes that I have loved since day one of moving to America. I didn't make this on a show, but I worked with its leftovers one day, and the result was something you could see in a Michelin-starred restaurant.

Place the leftover oatmeal in a glass container and make sure it's compact. Allow to cool down in the fridge overnight. The following day, remove the oatmeal from the container and onto a cutting board. Cut ¼-inch slices and sauté them in a lightly buttered skillet until nicely browned. Read the recipe to discover the toppings that go with it.

Preparation: 5 minutes
Cooking time: 10 minutes

2½ cups of water
½ cup of your favorite milk
1½ cup of old-fashioned rolled oats
¼ tsp. of salt
1 ripe banana
½ apple (grated)
¼ tsp. vanilla extract
Zest of ½ lemon and 1 orange
1 tsp. of honey
Cardamom, cloves, ginger, and cinnamon to taste

Mash the banana, grate the apple with a cheese grater, zest the citrus, and mix with the vanilla.

Bring the water and milk to a boil and add the salt, the banana mix, and the oats.

Cook until creamy, add the honey toward the end. Stir, allow to rest for a minute or two and serve hot with your favorite sprinkles or edible glitter. Catherine loves pink and purple. Add more honey or maple syrup if you like it sweeter. This oatmeal is not very sweet on purpose.

Toppings for the oatmeal leftover cakes:

1. Pistachios, cardamom, orange blossom, and honey: chop the pistachios and caramelize it with the other ingredients in a non-stick skillet for a few minutes at low heat (it burns easily, so always keep an eye on it).

2. Walnuts, vanilla, brown sugar, and cinnamon: same as above, but using brown sugar instead of honey.

3. Plantain chips, vanilla, honey, and lime: same as above, crush the plantain chips, squeeze some lime juice on a skillet, and caramelize. Plantain chips are savory and often salted, so you may want to add some powdered sugar to this topping when it has cooled down.

4. Peanuts, dry cranberries, rosemary, and honey: same as above, do not overdo with the rosemary.

RADICCHIO SALAD WITH KABOCHA SQUASH AND GOAT CHEESE

FOR 4 PEOPLE

This salad was born out of a leftover, but it turned out to be one of the most delicious warm meals of the autumn. The bitterness of the radicchio is beautiful with the sweetness of the squash and the earthy, deep flavor of the goat cheese, while the orange zest gives a fruity, fresh touch.

Preparation: 30 minutes
Cooking time: 1 hour

1 small head of radicchio
½ kabocha squash, with peel on
1 orange
1 cup of goat cheese
Extra-virgin olive oil, salt, pepper, and balsamic vinegar to taste
½ cup chopped pecans or walnuts (optional)

Pre-heat oven to 400°F.

Cut the kabocha in half, remove the seeds, and then quarter it.
Drizzle some extra-virgin olive oil on the kabocha, salt and place on a baking sheet. Cook for 45 minutes to 1 hour, until tender.

Meanwhile, clean the radicchio and slice it finely; you can fry some sage leaves and toast some pepitas here, to make this salad even more colorful and rich. Crumble the goat cheese, zest one orange, and add it to the radicchio.

When the kabocha is cooked and has cooled down enough to handle it, cube half of it and add to the salad (you can keep the rest for pasta, or cream, or simply eat it as is the following day. It keeps in the fridge for a few days in an airtight container).

Dress the salad with extra-virgin olive oil, salt, pepper, and balsamic vinegar.

Note: This salad is also delicious with the addition of some Italian farro or barley, simply cooked in salted boiling water, drained, and added to the dish once cooled down.

SUPERHERO'S MILK

FOR 25 FL.OZ. / 750 ML

I make this milk almost every morning for Catherine, and I stopped buying non-dairy milk altogether. She loves it, and I love to be able to know exactly what goes in her milk, no-sugar, or preservatives, and lots of fun in milking it together. This makes approximately ¾-liter bottle, and it keeps for 2-3 days in the fridge. It's also the milk I use in my tea and coffee daily. You can add honey or vanilla, if you wish, but I prefer to drink it unsweetened.

Preparation: 5 minutes

¼ cup raw, unsalted cashews
¾ cup old-fashioned rolled oats
½ tbsp. shredded coconut
1 tsp. pumpkin seeds
3 cups of water
  (*I blend it with 2 cups in my Ninja Bullet and then add more water*)
1 generous pinch of salt
Honey and vanilla (optional)

In a blender, add all the ingredients and 2 cups of water (the third cup you will add later).

Blend the ingredients for 15 seconds (don't blend too much because the oats will get slimy).

Filter the milk through a nut bag, then add the remaining water and pour into a milk bottle. Drink right away or keep in the fridge for 2-3 days.

Note: you can substitute cashews with almonds or walnuts (that will have to soak for at least 4 hours, then peeled). Have fun with it, and if you go for plain oat milk, use one cup of oats to 3 cups of water. Also, vanilla paste gives it a beautiful aroma. If you want it sweetened, add honey or maple syrup.

GRILLED LEEKS WITH FETA CHEESE

FOR 4 PEOPLE

This is an easy winter dishes that has a summer flair. I love leeks, and I love to grill pretty much any vegetable I have in the fridge. When you add the feta cheese, you make this a perfect entrée.

Preparation: 10 minutes
Cooking time: 15-20 minutes

12 leeks
1½ cup feta cheese
extra-virgin olive oil, salt, and pepper to taste
zest of 1 lemon
fresh herbs (dill, thyme, and rosemary)

Clean the leeks by removing the ends and the first 3 or 4 layers.
(Please see page 252 for a detailed description of how to clean leeks).
Boil the leeks in salted water for 10 minutes.

When they are fully cooked, drain them and squeeze out as much water as possible.
Grill the leeks on a hot cast iron grill (if inside) or on your outdoor grill until a few grill marks appear.

Crumble a quality feta cheese and set aside.

Arrange the grilled leeks on a serving plate and drizzle a generous amount of extra-virgin olive oil; add salt (or salt flakes if you have them) and pepper.

Sprinkle the feta cheese uniformly all over the leeks and sprinkle the finely minced fresh herbs and lemon zest. Enjoy warm with some good bread or crostini.

SMOKED PAPRIKA KALE CHIPS

FOR 4 PEOPLE

This has become my favorite way of eating kale, and Catherine can easily eat a whole bunch. After you make these once, you will never buy kale chips again.

Preparation: 10 minutes
Cooking time: 20-25 minutes

1 bunch of curly kale
Sea salt, extra-virgin olive oil, and smoked paprika to taste

Pre-heat oven to 275°F with convection on.

Thoroughly rinse the kale and remove leaves from the stem.

Spin it in a salad spinner and then pat dry with a towel. (It's very important to remove all the water from the leaves, so they can dry well in the oven and turn into chips.)

Once every leaf has been thoroughly dried, drizzle with extra-virgin olive oil and sprinkle with salt and as much smoked paprika as you wish. Massage kale with your hands to spread the condiment onto every leaf.

Arrange nicely spread out onto 2 baking sheets; it's important to leave enough space in-between the leaves for them to dry well.

Bake for 20-25 minutes, flipping the leaves after 10 or 15; they are ready when they are crunchy and transformed into real chips. Do not refrigerate as they tend to become soggy overnight.

CHICORY WITH OLIVES AND CAPERS

FOR 4 PEOPLE

This, to me, represents the essence of southern Italy. I love to use *puntarelle* chicory for this dish, but I know it's difficult to find here in the United States, so I made it with a mix of mustard greens, escarole, and dandelion, and the result was exceptional. I love this side vegetable as is, or with pasta.

Preparation: 10 minutes
Cooking time: 20 minutes

2 bunches of your favorite chicory or a mix of your favorites
2 cloves of garlic, whole
½ cup of capers
½ cup of Taggiasca olives, or Kalamata olives
Extra-virgin olive oil, salt, and chili flakes to taste
½ red onion

Rinse the chicory and chop the leaves in half.

Finely chop the onion.

Pit the olives and chop with the capers, then sauté with onion in extra-virgin olive oil, garlic, and chili flakes in a skillet for 5 minutes.

Blanch the chicory in salted water for 2-3 minutes, then drain and allow to rest on a bed of ice to preserve the color.

Add the chicory to capers and olives, lower the heat, cover the skillet with a lid and cook, slowly, for 10 minutes.

Remove garlic, salt, to taste. Drizzle more olive oil and serve hot.

LEMON-HONEY TOAST
WITH LAVENDER

FOR 4 PEOPLE

This recipe is one of my go-tos when I want something sweet, filling, and satisfying, without eating a real dessert. I love to make this toast with ciabatta bread or homemade sourdough. I prefer to use lemons with a thick, sweeter skin. And ultimately, I love lavender, but if you are not a fan you can substitute with rosemary or skip it altogether.

Preparation: 5 minutes
Cooking time: 20-25 minutes

1 organic lemon
4 slices of bread
Brown sugar, to taste
Honey, to taste
1 pinch of dry edible lavender flowers (optional)

Slice the lemon and sauté in a non-stick skillet with the sugar until nicely browned and caramelized (approximately 10 minutes).

Toast the bread to the desired level.

Arrange the caramelized lemon on the bread, sprinkle some lavender flowers, and drizzle with honey.

Enjoy warm.

The savory version of this toast is easy and equally delicious: sauté the lemon in a little olive oil or butter, do not sweeten. When ready, drizzle some oil on non-toasted bread and then arrange the lemon; sprinkle some salt and some finely chopped rosemary, top with plenty of shaved parmigiano, and toast the bread to desired level, so the cheese will slightly melt. This is also a beautiful topping for a flatbread or a pizza.

ALMOND RICOTTA TRUFFLES WITH COCONUT AND LIME

FOR 15 TRUFFLES

These truffles were one of the earliest recipes we made on the show, together with the chocolate and date truffles (next recipe). They are a beautiful, fresh, and creative vegan dessert that will surprise your guests, or make your day a little brighter, a little sweeter, a little better.

Preparation: 20-25 minutes
Passive time: 1 hour

1 pack of Kite Hill almond ricotta
1 cup unsweetened shredded coconut
¼ tsp. vanilla extract
3 tbsp. powdered sugar
2 limes (zest)

In a mixing bowl, mix ricotta, powdered sugar, vanilla, and shredded coconut. Refrigerate the mix for at least 1 hour. You can make this mix the night before, rolling the truffles when ready to serve. The longer the mix stays in the fridge, the easier it will be to keep it together and roll the truffles.

Delicately roll the little truffles in your hands and then coat them by rolling them a mixture of shredded coconut and lime zest. Refrigerate for 1 hour and enjoy chilled.

COCOA AND DATE TRUFFLES

FOR 20 TRUFFLES

These truffles are decadent, rich, and sexy. Perfect for a party, or for those moments during the day when you need both an indulgence and a pick-me-up. What I love about this recipe is that you can apply the base of the truffle and dress it up for Christmas, for example, with a crunchy coating of peppermint stick or caramelized sesame, or for the summer, perhaps, with a coating of coconut, or chopped almonds. They make a beautiful gift or party favor, and they are very easy to make.

Preparation: 30 minutes
Passive time: 1 hour

5 tbsp. unsweetened raw baking cacao
17 whole small Medjool dates, pitted (14-15 if they are bigger)
2 tbsp. hazelnut oil
½ tsp. vanilla extract
½ cup unsalted cashews
1 pinch sea salt
½ cup of sesame seeds
1 tbsp. of brown sugar

Toast and caramelize the sesame seeds in a skillet with brown sugar, at low-medium heat.

When they are toasted (approximately 5 minutes), remove from the heat and from the skillet and allow to completely cool down. Set aside while you prepare the truffles.

Place all the ingredients in the food processor and pulse until the dough turns into a thick paste. Slowly add more oil if necessary. The dough should be pasty, dry, but malleable enough to be molded into 2-inch round truffles.

Move the dough onto a clean plate and form the little truffle balls.

On a clean plate, prepare the sesame seed coating and delicately roll every truffle in it. Refrigerate for at least 30 minutes, possibly 1 hour.

BLACK BEAN SALAD WITH CHERRY TOMATOES AND BALSAMIC VINAIGRETTE

FOR 2 PEOPLE

Another early recipe from the show, this salad is made with organic canned beans because—for as much as we try to eat fresh and local—sometimes life just doesn't allow it. And I am a huge fan of organic canned beans of every kind. They make amazing pasta, soups, salads, and vegan burgers.

Preparation: 20 minutes

1 can organic black beans
1 cup organic cherry tomatoes
¼ cup shaved parmesan cheese
1 tbsp. fresh or dry chives
2-3 leaves of fresh basil
Balsamic reduction (optional)
Extra-virgin olive oil, balsamic vinegar, salt, and pepper to taste
(I love to use salt flakes on this salad)

Rinse the beans and place them in a medium salad bowl.

Chop the cherry tomatoes, shave the cheese, and add to the beans. Chop the herbs and add to the salad.

Dress the salad a few minutes before serving so it doesn't become soggy. Add a good extra-virgin olive oil, balsamic reduction, and vinegar (the reduction gives a beautiful sweetness to the salad) salt and pepper to taste. Be creative with the dressing; add as much/little of it as you like.

SOUPS, SAUCES, DIPS, AND STEWS THAT TASTE LIKE HOME

WHAT DOES HOME TASTE LIKE?

s there a flavor or a scent that reminds you of where you are from?

One summer day in 2019, I was driving back to the valley from Los Feliz in particularly bad traffic, and the temperature had, by 2:30 PM, reached 110°F.

The day had started awfully. Ben and I had had a fight because I had lashed out in anger for something there was nothing to be angry about. By now, I know that my anger is not about anger; it hides my fear, my frustration, and my anxiety about every task in life, from building a gate around our new house to deciding what to have for dinner or buying a pair of shoes. And yet, that day, I gave in and allowed anger to take over.

Later in the afternoon, after talking to a friend about what had happened, I felt so ashamed of my behavior that I didn't want to return home. I owed Ben an amend, and I wasn't ready to face him. So, on that blazing day, I decided to drive all the way to Chatsworth (not at all on my route, for those of you not familiar with the geography of Southern California) to return three onesies I had bought for Catherine on Amazon.

During that very long drive, I listened to my Italian playlist on Tidal: Antonello Venditti, Francesco De Gregori, Fabrizio De Andrè, Tiromancino, and Loredana Bertè. When Gianna Nannini's *Un'Estate Italiana* (an Italian summer) played, I had goosebumps; I felt a knot in my chest, and I began to think about Italy in the summer.

The song, which is something of a second Italian national anthem, was composed by Giorgio Moroder for the 1990 FIFA World Cup, which was held in Italy. But the version that every Italian knows, and loves, is the one whose lyrics were written by singer-songwriter Gianna Nannini.

I had tried to write several essays about Italy before, but I could never get myself to start because, for a long time, I felt resentful of it. Italy, a whole country, yes.

"When are they going to realize how much I have achieved abroad?" I had asked myself countless times.

I hurt because nobody other than a few journalists from my hometown had recognized me and my work. I hurt because I had always wanted to make my country proud, and I couldn't understand what I had to do for Italy to shine a light on me like it did for other, more famous, expatriates.

After a few years in Los Angeles, therefore, I cut ties with my roots. I tried to hide my accent, thankfully never succeeding, and I Americanized the pronunciation of my first and last name. I felt betrayed; I was angry and disappointed, and I wanted to forget about Italy.

But things changed when I got sober and worked on my resentments. I understood that Italy had been, in a way, a metaphor: I wanted my parents to be proud of me, I wanted the people I had left in Italy to finally see me and consider me special. It was never about the country; it was about a wounded ego.

I don't think I could live there again. California is the place I call home now, but I've been missing where I'm from a lot, since becoming a mother: I miss my native language, the scents, the food, the seasons.

One day, Catherine and I were returning home after a beautiful afternoon at the beach. She often gets carsick, and on narrow and winding Topanga Canyon, she cried and screamed until I played Antonello Venditti's song "Notte Prima degli Esami" (another classic that every Italian knows and sings along with, remembering with nostalgia the final exam of high school, *maturità*). The song is filled with so many cultural references that it's easy to feel like a proud Italian when listening to it, and Catherine's smile in response to it moved me to tears.

That's how this essay became an ode to Italy, and ode to a good, old Italian summer.

"Is there a flavor that reminds you of where you are from?"

Grilled fish and grilled bread are synonymous with Italian summer to me. There is something about the burned crust of a ciabatta bread with fresh basil, tomato, and extra-virgin olive oil drizzled on top that makes everything okay. The play between crunchy, buttery, and tangy makes me want to sit down, relax, do nothing, living la dolce vita.

I never relax. I never "do nothing." I am uncomfortable in stillness.

The smell of a freshly sliced cantaloupe also reminds me of summer in Italy, with some San Daniele prosciutto crudo (dry-cured ham) and breadsticks. What more do you need to start your meal with a smile? Imagine yourself in the backyard of a rustic little house; it's hot, humid, and you are sitting at the table with your family. There is bread, two glass bottles, one with water, and one with red wine. You cut the melon, take a bite with a slice of prosciutto, and let go. Summer at last!

Fennel seed reminds me of July in Puglia, a region in the south-east of the country, the heel of the boot, as they say. My father was born there, and with his parents, he moved to Avigliana, in Piemonte, when he was 5 years old. It was three years after the end of the war, and like many families in those times, they migrated north in search of a better life. So, when I was a child, we would spend part of the summer visiting his family who had stayed in the south, both in Bari, the capital, and Spinazzola, a nearby small town.

My paternal grandmother still uses fennel seed a lot in her food. I use it in my tomato sauce, at times, in my vegan meatballs, and when I make taralli.

When I taste fennel seed, I imagine red soil, hot and dry. I see people walking down the street in tank tops that are a little too tight, and slippers; they're sweaty, never in a hurry. They carry bread and "caroselli" cucumbers (a variety of muskmelon autochthonous of the region of Puglia), they complain about the heat, about the too-long line at the post office, and about the government, of course. But when they arrive home, they slice the caroselli and eat them with fennel seed taralli and a glass of homemade red wine. There is a tablecloth on the table; the windows are open because there is no air conditioning, and from the narrow balcony you can see the neighbors across the small courtyard preparing their lunch. The TV is on, and so is the fan that is the only source of breeze in the entire house.

More than any other season, summer reminds me of Italy. I think it's because during summer people go out more, they become more social, more relaxed, and I can more easily observe them, their movements, their faces, the decisions they make.

I don't remember much about my childhood, but I remember the details of where I have been; I remember the smells, and I remember how the people around me interacted with each other and with myself. I don't remember the interaction itself, but I remember how it made me feel.

Gelato is synonymous with Italian summer, but even more so is anise-flavored popsicle, or the mint one; mint popsicles are so refreshing that they clear your head and makes room for more to remember.

And I remember a man named Calogero, in the 1990s, when I attended middle school. He sold popsicles outside the school on his orange Piaggio Ape. We all loved him so much! I remember every flavor: lemon, strawberry, orange, Coca Cola, anise, mint... that's all he sold, and we couldn't wait to get off school and have a "*ghiacciolo*" (popsicle) from Calogero.

Memories like these make me feel alive.

"Does any of this make sense to you?"

Italian summer means the beaches of Liguria, pasta with pesto, and white wine that has remained in the fridge for just the right amount of time. Italian summer is music competitions on TV, miniskirts, strolls on the main drag, open windows until late night, and 9:00 pm dinners in lieu of the wintry 7:30, or 19:30, as we say there.

I look forward to the day when Ben, Catherine, and I will spend the summer in Italy. They will experience their first *Ferragosto* in Italy, on the 15 of August, when Italians celebrate summer with grand barbecues and parties, fireworks, watermelon, and music all through the night. We will visit the riviera, or Forte dei Marmi, in Tuscany; we will have ice cream by the beach. My favorite is a vanilla stick with a heart of sour black cherry, covered in dark chocolate and hazelnut praline. We will eat watermelon at midnight and spit the seeds into a pasta plate left from the late dinner.

"Do you ever get goosebumps when you think about your native land?" I have been thinking about it more and more lately, as I witness the increasing number of migrant families and children from South America at the American border, running away from their summers.

Guatemalan summers...what do they look like?

What are the memories that refugees carry with them? Syrian summers, Salvadoran summers, Mexican summers; what will these families remember about them?

I am lucky to be able to re-experience my Italian summer any time I want. I came to America by choice, not out of necessity. When I left my country, I was ready to embrace the new one, to learn a new language, and to adopt new habits. I was ready to fall in love with Thanksgiving dinner, and with the fireworks on the 4th of July.

But refugees and migrants are not ready. They will forever miss the scent of summer on their native soil, and they won't, very likely, ever experience it again. Can you imagine the horror they are escaping to sacrifice such a sacred feeling? It is out of respect for those who, to have a chance at life, have been forced to eradicate their roots that today I honor mine.

I feel alive when I think of an Italian summer, and I dedicate this ode to all the people who feel the same about their native land, with the wish they may, one day, taste again the summer of when they were a child.

CREAMY MUSHROOM SOUP WITH HERBED CROSTINI

This, to me, tastes like home. This *vellutata*, traditional French soup that contains heavy cream and that is smooth like velvet (hence the name, velvety soup), holds all the autumn flavor of the Aosta Valley. My grandparents and I would always go mushroom picking at the end of August, and this warm soup is perfect for cooking your favorite mushrooms. This is my kind of comfort food—easy, nutritious, with a story, and full of flavor.

Preparation: 15 minutes
Cooking time: 25 minutes for the broth and 35 minutes for the soup

1 pound of mixed mushrooms (white, brown, chanterelle)
2 shallots
3 small potatoes
4 cups vegetable broth (you may have to add a bit more or reduce the quantity according the type of potatoes, or desired consistency)
Fresh herbs (thyme, basil, chives, sage, rosemary,)
½ cup or more parmesan cheese or pecorino cheese
2 tbsp. of heavy cream (or to taste); for alternatives you can use milk or oat milk
Extra-virgin olive oil, salt, and pepper to taste

Sauté mushrooms, thinly sliced potatoes, and thinly sliced shallot (I use a mandolin for this) in extra-virgin olive oil, stirring, and then add the vegetable broth and the herbs.

Cook, stirring occasionally, for 30-40 minutes (or more, if you have the time).
Add cream and cook for 5 more minutes.

Adjust salt and pepper and blend with an immersion blender until smooth and creamy.
Add cream and broth if necessary.

Serve with generous grated parmesan or pecorino cheese and a drizzle of olive oil.

Crostini:

½ French baguette
Fresh herbs
Olive oil
Sea salt

Cut the bread into small cubes, mince the herbs. Sauté bread in olive oil until nicely gold and crunchy. Now add the herbs, salt, and pepper and serve warm with your soup.

PRESSURE COOKER BEANS

FOR 6-8 PEOPLE; TRY SERVING WITH PASTA OR CHILI

This is a basic recipe for the preparation of any dry bean. I love them all, but I would never stop eating black-eyed peas. For many years I was terrified of the pressure cooker. I never even owned one, and I remember walking precariously around the kitchen when my mom used it (quite often). Then, one day, I saw that Ben owned one and I decided to give it a try, with beans. I usually make a big pot and freeze whatever we don't eat on cooking day.

Preparation: 6 hours for soaking the dry beans
Cooking time: 20 minutes from the whistle

500 gr. (17.6 oz. or approximately 2¾ cups) of dry beans
1 carrot
1 small onion
1 stick of celery
1 or 2 chopped tomatoes (or some tomato paste or tomato sauce)
1 bay leaf
1 sprig of fresh rosemary
1 sprig of fresh thyme
Extra-virgin olive oil, salt, and pepper to taste
Chili flakes (optional)

Soak the beans in cold water for 6 hours or overnight.
Rinse and clean the vegetables.

Drizzle some extra-virgin olive oil in your pressure cooker, then add all the ingredients but the salt. Add 4-5 cups of water. You can add a little more water if you want more of a soupy result.

Safely tighten the pressure cooker and place on medium-high heat until it starts whistling.
Lower the heat and cook for 20 minutes from the whistle.

Turn off the heat and do not open until the pressure cooker is completely silent.
Open the pressure cooker, remove the vegetables and the herbs, add salt and pepper to taste and use the beans for your desired preparation.

You can cook the beans for 15 minutes for a firmer taste.
To make a fantastic vegan chili, sauté some Boca vegan crumbs in extra-virgin olive oil. When they are completely thawed, add the beans and simmer for 5-10 minutes. Add salt to taste and chili flakes.
It's truly amazing!

ZUCCHINI AND POTATO SOUP

FOR 6 PEOPLE

Like the other zucchini recipes, this one could have been in the section of this book dedicated to my mother. But, like we all do, when I think about my mom's cooking, I think of home. There is something beautiful about zucchini and potatoes, a touch of butter, and some pasta. This soup will forever be a classic for me, a classic Mom taught me how to make.

Preparation: 15 minutes
Cooking time: 2 hours

4 Italian zucchinis
2 big yellow potatoes or 3 medium-small ones
300 gr. (10.6 oz.) of short pasta (*I like farfalline or elbow pasta for this*)
1 tsp of unsalted butter
1 bay leaf
1 onion
1 carrot
1 clove of garlic
1 pinch of palm sugar
1 stick of celery
Extra-virgin olive oil, salt, and pepper to taste
½ cup grated parmigiano cheese
Fresh thyme to taste

Prepare the broth by boiling onion, carrot, bay leaf, garlic, and celery for 1 hour or so. Meanwhile, dice the zucchini and the potatoes to bite-size.

When the vegetables are soft and cooked through, remove them from the water.

Add the zucchini and the potatoes to the broth, as well as a light drizzle of extra-virgin olive oil, a pinch of palm sugar, a generous pinch of salt, and a small sprig of fresh thyme; cook for 15-20 minutes.

Add the pasta, salt to taste if necessary, and add the fresh thyme.

When the pasta is cooked, 10 minutes approximately, add the butter and remove from the heat. Allow to rest for 10 minutes before serving with freshly grated parmigiano cheese.

BELL PEPPERS WITH POTATOES, TOMATOES, AND FRESH BASIL

FOR 4 PEOPLE

This simple recipe comes from my paternal grandmother, and it's so beautiful that I wish I weren't the only one in my family to eat bell peppers. Ben, in fact, is allergic, and Catherine has not shown signs of enjoyment, when trying it.

I love when recipes have only a few ingredients; it means they are packed with flavor. And this one is no different.

Preparation: 10 minutes
Cooking time: 1 hour

4 bell peppers: red, yellow, orange, and green
4 medium yellow potatoes
1 clove of garlic, whole
1-2 ripe tomatoes
5-6 leaves of fresh basil
Salt, pepper, and extra-virgin olive oil to taste
1 pinch of palm sugar or brown sugar

Steam the potatoes and peel them; set aside.

Clean the bell peppers by rinsing them and by removing all the seeds.

Cut the bell peppers in 1-inch squares (approximately).

Sauté garlic in extra-virgin olive oil for 1 minute in a skillet, then add the bell peppers.

Lower the heat and cook until they become soft. Add 1 pinch of palm sugar and salt to taste. Stir regularly to prevent from sticking.

While the bell peppers cook, dice the tomatoes, and chop the basil.

When the bell peppers are cooked, break the potatoes with your hands (very important my grandmother says, do not use a knife) and add them to the bell peppers. Stir and salt to taste, cook for 5 minutes adding more oil if necessary.

Transfer the bell peppers and the potatoes to a serving bowl, add the tomatoes and the fresh basil, and serve.

MY TOMATO SAUCE

FOR A BIG POT

I never liked canned tomato sauce, as I find there is always too much garlic, or added flavors that, to me, have nothing to do with fresh sauce. It's very easy to make a beautiful sauce; it takes few ingredients and just a bit of patience. You can, like I do, make a big batch, and then freeze what you don't use right away.

Cooking time: 3-4 hours

1 shallot (optional)
3 cans of San Marzano tomato pulp or tomato pulp, a quality one
1 bottle (approximately 24 oz.) of tomato purée (passata)
1 tsp. brown sugar
1 tbsp. of extra-virgin olive oil
4-6 leaves of fresh basil

Finely chop the shallot, and sauté in a medium/big pot with the olive oil. Add all the tomatoes, 1.2 cup of water, sugar, and basil. Stir, and let simmer to medium heat for 1-2 hour. Stir regularly to prevent from sticking.

After one hour, add salt to taste. The more you cook the sauce the better the tomato tastes and loses its acidity. If I have time, I cook my sauce for up to 3 or 4 hours. Tomato sauce is a labor of love; it's not difficult to make and doesn't require your constant attention until ready.

SPINACH, RICE, AND POTATO SOUP

FOR 6 PEOPLE

My grandmother would make this simple soup a lot, I love the combination of spinach and potatoes. The only difference from the original one she used to make is a squeeze of lime juice (we didn't know what a lime was, since we didn't have limes in the Alps). Why? After making it, I realized it missed something, a touch of acidity; I thought of Thai soups, which often have lime in them, and I gave it a try. It was one of the best soups I have ever had in my life. Also, it's super quick to make. I prepared it after returning from a solo vacation in Ojai[10] in only 1 hour.

Preparation: 10 minutes
Cooking 50 minutes

4-5 cups vegetable broth (recipe and ingredients below)
1 bunch of spinach
4 small potatoes
1-2 tbsp. unsalted butter
1½ cup of arborio rice
1 pinch of nutmeg
½ lime
Salt and pepper to taste
2 parmesan rinds (*when I don't have any, I like to grate some parmesan cheese in the soup while it cooks*)

For the vegetable broth:

2 zucchini
2 carrots
1 stick of celery
1 onion
2 bay leaves
fresh herbs to taste (rosemary, thyme, basil, chives, and sage)
Any top or bottom of vegetables you have (*I usually freeze the fennel tops with the asparagus bottoms, and any vegetable scrap I don't use for cooking. This way, I always have vegetables for a quick broth, and I reduce the waste to almost zero*).

To prepare the broth, place the rinsed vegetables and herbs in the pressure cooker, fill with water and cook for 20-25 minutes from the whistle.

Rinse the spinach and chop it finely.

Sauté the spinach with the butter for a few minutes. Then add the potatoes, peeled and cubed. Add the broth and cook for 5 minutes, then add the rice and the parmesan rinds (or the grated cheese if you don't have them), and cook for 30-35 minutes.

---

10 *Small, beautiful town one hour and a half from Los Angeles, where there is a beautiful resort. It was the first time taking time off and actually "traveling" by myself since I married Ben.*

Taste the soup, salt to taste, and squeeze in the lime.

Serve with plenty of grated parmesan cheese. This soup is fantastic the following day and it can be frozen for up to 1 month.

CREAMY PEA SOUP

FOR 6 PEOPLE

This dish is similar to the mushroom soup, but made with frozen peas instead, and with a small change in the choice of fresh herbs (mint goes beautifully with peas). You could never tell this is made with frozen vegetables, and neither will your guests. With the recipe, you can present a beautifully French-inspired dish that you can find at some of the best gourmet restaurants all over Europe.

Preparation: 10 minutes
Cooking time: 25 minutes for the broth and 30-40 minutes for the soup

2 bags of frozen peas
2 small shallots
3 small potatoes
3-4 cups vegetable broth
Fresh herbs (thyme, basil, chives, sage, rosemary, mint)
2 parmesan rinds (optional)
½ cup or more parmesan cheese or pecorino cheese
2 tbsp. of heavy cream (or to taste) or as an alternative you can use milk or oat milk
Extra-virgin olive oil, salt, and pepper to taste

Sauté peas, thinly sliced potatoes, and thinly sliced shallot (I use a mandolin for this) in extra-virgin olive oil, stirring, and then add the vegetable broth and the herbs with the parmesan crust (if you have it).

Cook, stirring occasionally, for 30-40 minutes (or more, if you have the time).

Add cream and cook for 5 more minutes.

Adjust salt and pepper and blend with an immersion blender until smooth and creamy.

Sample the soup, add salt to taste, and squeeze in the lime. The rind is a treat, and I love to be surprised finding one in my soup. Alternatively, you can serve on a small plate or eat it hot, straight out of the pot, chewy and delicious.

Add cream and broth if necessary.

Serve with generous grated parmesan or pecorino cheese and a drizzle of olive oil.

CREAMY VEGETABLE SOUP (PASSATO DI VERDURE)

FOR 6 PEOPLE

This is a very simple and healthy soup that I made on Instagram on a day of extreme physical discomfort. I had put some jeans on and that day they felt tight. I hate the feeling of feeling my body, and that day I felt every cell. But instead of using the old coping mechanism of hiding and hurting myself, I kept the jeans on and turned the camera on. I recorded a video for Instagram of making the soup and I told my community how I felt and how uncomfortable I was. Every time I share my pain or discomfort, the old voice in my head becomes more and more of a whisper, and I find a little bit more freedom and peace of mind. This soup is comforting, delicious, and at every bite, you feel the care you are taking of yourself and of your body.

Preparation: 10 minutes
Cooking time: 60-90 minutes

3-4 carrots
3 sticks of celery
3 leeks
½ onion
½ kabocha squash or butternut squash
3-4 medium potatoes
2 asparagus (*I used the end of asparagus I had frozen, instead of throwing them away. I also had frozen fennel tops, and added them to the soup.*)
½ cup frozen peas
1 zucchini
½ cup of spinach or broccoli leaves, or kale
1 bay leaf
A touch of turmeric
Extra-virgin olive oil, salt, sweet soy sauce, and pepper to taste
2 tbsp. of milk or heavy cream, or crème fraîche (optional)

Rinse all the vegetables, peel squash, and remove bottoms from leeks as well as the first two layers. Now, peel potatoes, carrots, and onions.

Chop every vegetable roughly and place them in a big pot with some extra-virgin olive oil a mix of fresh herbs (I have used rosemary, basil, chives, thyme, and sage).

Sauté for 5 minutes and then add just enough water to cover the vegetables.

Bring to a boil and then simmer for 1-2 hours, covered, and stirring occasionally.

When all the vegetables are nicely cooked, add some turmeric and sweet soy sauce (I highly recommend always having some in the house, as it gives a magical flavor to anything you cook).

Now, with an immersion blender, blend the soup to a velvety cream and pass the soup through a strainer to get rid of any residual leeks and asparagus.
Salt to taste and serve hot with plenty of parmesan cheese.

Note: Every time I clean vegetables, I don't throw away tops and bottoms, outer leaves, or less delicate parts. I rinse everything well and I freeze it all. I use all the discards every time I need to make vegetable broth: broccoli stems and leaves, fennel and carrot tops, asparagus bottoms, fennel outer leaves. They will make an amazing broth and will reduce the waste. It's a win-win.

FRESH FAVA BEAN PURÉE

FOR 4 PEOPLE

This recipe is very easy and so delicious that it can be eaten with a spoon out of the jar. I usually make it for pasta, but I always make extra and use it as a spread, or for a creamy snack whenever I am hungry for something healthy.

Preparation: 20 minutes
Cooking time: 5 minutes

3½ pounds of fresh fava beans (weight is for unshelled beans)
½ cup of freshly grated pecorino cheese
Salt, extra-virgin olive oil and pepper to taste
5 leaves of fresh basil
Chives and thyme to taste

Shell the fava beans.

Boil the shelled fava beans for 3-4 minutes in salted water, then drain them.

Remove the peel from the boiled fava beans as soon as they have cooled down enough to handle. Grate the pecorino cheese.

In the glass of a hand mixer, combine the cheese, the fresh herbs, the shelled fava beans, a light drizzle of oil, some salt, and pepper.

Purée the fava beans and add some water if necessary.

Adjust salt and pepper and either use for pasta sauce, a bruschetta spread, or a dip. You can keep it in the fridge in a jar for 2 or 3 days.

PREGNANCY AND
EATING DISORDERS

from 2017

didn't know that, with the joy of my much-longed-for pregnancy, the horror of my bulimia and anorexia could come back so violently after three years of healing: with a vengeance, actually, despite intense and life-changing therapy sessions, sobriety, a happy marriage, and especially despite my newly found love for food and cooking.

But it did happen. And my first trimester has been, almost secretly, one of the most difficult times I have ever been through in my life.

I am 21 weeks pregnant today, and I am writing this from the living room of my home in Tarzana, California. The sun is setting, and the beautiful view from the garden over the San Fernando Valley keeps me company while Ben, my husband, is on tour with the band. After being on the road with him for weeks, I had to take a break, and take care of myself, and the baby, at home.

I knew that the first trimester could be rough, with all-day morning sickness that doesn't magically disappear when the clock strikes twelve noon, and with fatigue, and discomfort on top of that. And yet I didn't know the extent to which my inability to accept the changes that my body was quickly going through, as well as the difficulty in finding healthy food that I could eat, would turn my experience of the tour into a struggling tour de force. I was six-and-a-half weeks pregnant when we landed in Dallas; then we flew to New Orleans (city of magic and mystery, not so easy to enjoy when newly pregnant and sensitive to every smell), Orlando, and ultimately to Chicago, where the idea for this essay came about, and where I hit my bottom. I was nine weeks pregnant when we arrived in Chicago, and perhaps because of the hormones that I had been taking for months before our several fertility treatments, perhaps because of the progesterone supplement that I had been prescribed after the last procedure, or perhaps because of how my body genetically reacted to pregnancy, I was gaining a lot of weight. I was gaining weight so fast that—even though rationally I had been ready for pregnancy for quite a while—my eyes, my brain, my heart, and my soul were not.

So instead of seeing a pregnant woman reflected in the mirror of Suite 1334, I saw the seventeen-year-old me: an overweight young girl with long chestnut hair, full of crazy dreams and creative ideas, and yet a young girl who had just begun the devastating practice of starving, binging, and throwing up.

"What kind of mother will I be? I shouldn't have a child," I cried myself to sleep one night. Ben was performing in Memphis, Tennessee, and I had stayed behind; I couldn't deal with more hit-or-miss backstage food. I was tired, and most of all, I felt ashamed. I felt as if I couldn't share my pain because "that's not what a mother would do," especially when friends and family knew how much I wanted *to be* pregnant, and how hard we had tried in the past year and a half. I was lost.

Moreover, I missed cooking my own food and sharing it with our friends. I longed for the comfort I had grown accustomed to in my kitchen. I missed home and the healthy life I had in California; I missed the old me, the Alice of nine weeks before.

In fact, from one day to another, *I* as I knew myself had vanished—my body had been taken over by the future baby, and the teenage Alice had replaced the adult one.

"I can't even look at myself in the mirror," I told my therapists, in tears, during a Skype session from Chicago. "I can't touch my skin; I don't recognize myself." I cried the entire hour, and for the first time I had the courage to tell them: "I gained 15 pounds in nine weeks, do you understand?" Just the sound of that number made me cringe. I felt embarrassed and humiliated. I was creating life in my uterus, but, surrounded by the luxury of one of the most elegant hotels in the city, I longed for death.

"I wish there was something I could do, my love," Ben said to me one evening, with beautiful peach-colored roses in his hands. "I hate seeing you like this." Every day he'd talk to our baby through the blue cotton of my pajamas, thoughtfully not touching nor uncovering my bloated belly. Not one day went by without him saying: "You are the most beautiful woman I have ever seen." I, protected by the blue cotton of my pajamas, hated my bloated belly, my disappearing waist, and my chubby arms, once slender and toned. Even my face looked different.

The weather was quite cold in Chicago in those days. My old clothes started to feel uncomfortable, so I folded away my skinny jeans. I didn't go out but spent five days watching the windy city moving fast and feeling the renewal of spring, while there, on the 13th floor where I was, it felt like autumn was giving way to winter.

When we returned to Los Angeles, after three weeks on the road, I refused to go out for days, save for quick runs to the local Whole Foods, and to the gym. I wanted to lose some of the weight before being seen out and about. I was in denial of my pregnancy: To my eyes, I was fat. I never even wanted to see my friends because I was afraid of their shocked reaction: "Oh my God, she is huge. What happened to her? I bet now she'll stop making all that pasta!" I pictured them saying behind my back.

"I always admired your pregnancy," I told my dear friend Marthe, one afternoon over the phone.

Marthe is the mom of a beautiful 10-month-old, and when she was pregnant, Ben and I were undergoing fertility treatment. It was a challenging time for us as a couple, and for me as a woman, and Marthe was an inspiration to me, a source of hope. I always thought she was beautiful, and that she had gained the perfect amount of weight. "How did you do it? I mean, you gained what...20?" I had promised myself I would be just like her, were I to be blessed with a child.

"Are you kidding?" she said. I could perceive her gentle and genuine smile as she said: "I gained 50 pounds! But I was okay with it, and my doctor wasn't worried at all."

I remained silent.

After I hung up the phone, I went out and sat for a while in the garden, near the rosemary and the aromatic herbs, very confused. It was a beautiful summer late afternoon in Tarzana; the sun was shining, and a pleasant breeze was blowing. I closed my eyes, and for the first time I clearly saw what I had not been able to even notice until that moment.

My eating disorder had made me so blind that 50 pounds on another woman looked to me like 20. So, after learning about Marthe's pregnancy weight, I began to search Google for images of pregnant actresses.

"What do you see when you look at Rachel Bilson?" my therapist asked. She looked at me with love and compassion. I didn't feel judged. This time, the session took place in her studio, in Beverly Hills. I wore black maternity leggings and a black blouse—a big scarf covered me as if it were a blanket as I sat on the couch in front of her.

"A beautiful pregnant woman," I said. "But I'm starting to think I will never see myself that way." I re-experienced the humiliation of the 17-year-old me after being bullied in school, and the shame she felt after looking at a photo of her and seeing someone she didn't recognize. "That can't be me," I recalled the voice of young Alice saying.

I felt her sorrow. I felt her unhappiness and her discomfort, and I felt her anger. But I also felt compassion for her.

In these past three years of healing, I have made progress with my eating disorder. And thanks to two fantastic doctors who truly care, I have also begun to cook; I have discovered happiness in the kitchen by embracing my Italian roots to the fullest, and by bringing back to life memories of my grandmother, of my childhood, in the form of delicious recipes. In these past three years, I haven't thrown up or starved myself, and yet I have not made peace with that teenage girl who hated herself so much that she hurt and tried to destroy her body for years.

I am still pregnant, so my body keeps changing daily. I stopped the progesterone, but I am in my second trimester now, and I will gain weight.

"You are pregnant, Alice. You are going to be a mother," I say to myself every day when I get dressed and face my naked body in the mirror. And that is not 17-year-old Alice speaking. It is me today.

It means I must have found the first little piece of my lost self.

I shared this story because I don't want women to suffer in silence while admiring fragments of life on social media, where everything looks perfect, beautiful, and like a movie. There is no shame in living real life as real women, with all that being a real woman entails.

RECIPES INSPIRED
BY MY MOM

ZUCCHINI IN GARDEN CRUST

FOR 4 PEOPLE

I don't know why, but zucchini is one of the vegetables that most reminds me of both my grand-mother and of my mother, especially the lighter colored ones that are sweeter and don't leave the bitter after taste that is typical of the darker variety. Try and think if there is a vegetable that takes you back to your childhood; we have often talked about this on the show, and I find a beautiful way to reconnect with our ancestors, and perhaps rediscover old recipes.

This one is very easy to make, quick, also, and full of spring and summer flavor. You can per-sonalize this crust with any nut or herb you like/ have in your pantry, and you can add it to pretty much any vegetable, from zucchinis to broccoli, bell peppers and eggplants or even carrots, mush-rooms, and potatoes, as well as fish.

Preparation: 10-15 minutes
Cooking time: 15 minutes + 25 minutes

6 Italian zucchinis
1 small sprig of rosemary
fresh basil, thyme, dill, mint, chives to taste,
        a generous handful in total, according to your taste
2 tbsp. of raw unsalted almonds
2 tbsp. of walnuts
1 tsp. of hemp seeds (optional)
140 gr. (5 oz. or approximately 1½ cup) of breadcrumbs
¼cup of parmesan cheese
¼ cup of pecorino cheese
Salt, extra-virgin olive oil and pepper to taste
1 pinch of coconut sugar

In a food processor, mix all dry ingredients except zucchini, and pulse until small crumbs form.

Slice the zucchinis in quarters, then place them in a baking dish and drizzle them with olive oil.

Add salt and pepper and cover with plenty of garden crust. (Save the rest for other preparations. I keep mine in a jar, in the fridge, and it lasts up to 2 weeks).

Bake the zucchinis for 20-25 minutes at 400°F.

Enjoy warm, or at room temperature. These are amazing the day after as well.

GRILLED ZUCCHINI PARMIGIANA

FOR 4-6 PEOPLE

My mom doesn't fry food. She never has; she never will. I hated it when I was a child, but now I am grateful she taught me how to make delicious food that is also healthy and good for us. That's why this dish is in the section dedicated to her, because every time that I have the option of either grilling or frying something, I always follow my mom's lead and take out the grill.

Preparation: 30-40 minutes
Cooking time: 40-45 minutes
Passive time: 10 minutes

12 zucchinis
200 gr. (7 oz.) of fontina, asiago, or provolone cheese
150 gr. (5.3 oz. or approximately 1¾ cup) of grated parmesan cheese
200 gr. (7 oz. or approximately 1 cup) of tomato sauce
5-6 leaves fresh basil
Extra-virgin olive oil, salt, and pepper to taste

Rinse zucchinis, slice them lengthwise, ¼-inch thin.

Grill zucchinis for a few minutes on both sides. Continue for all the zucchinis you have. While they grill, chop the cheese in small cubes and grate the parmesan or pecorino cheese.

When the zucchinis are cooked, start layering them with cheese and sauce. Start by putting some tomato sauce on the bottom of your baking dish, then arrange zucchinis, salt, add more sauce, sprinkle parmesan cheese, and add the chopped cheese. Repeat until you have finished all the zucchinis and finish the last layer with tomato sauce and grated parmesan cheese.

Bake for 40-45 minutes to 425°F with convection on.

Allow to rest for 5-10 minutes and enjoy!

Note: This dish is even better on the second or third day. I like to serve it with a simple salad and plenty of bread for scarpetta!

STEAMED ZUCCHINI WITH PARMESAN CHEESE

FOR 4 PEOPLE, AS A SIDE DISH

This last zucchini recipe is one that my mom makes all the time, and that for a long time I had forgotten. I made it for Ben for the first time during the pandemic, and with the first bite, I went back to being a child…and I was happy. Do not be taken aback by the simplicity of both ingredients and directions: this is truly a perfect recipe to really taste the zucchinis. This dish can be an appetizer, a side dish, or an entrée, according to the quantities.

Preparation: 10 minutes
Cooking time: 10-15 minutes

6 medium zucchinis
150 gr. (5.3 oz. or approximately 1¾ cup) of parmesan cheese (or more, to taste)
Extra-virgin olive oil, salt, and pepper to taste

Rinse the zucchinis, cut them lengthwise and steam them for 10-15 minutes. They should be soft but still able to hold their shape.

While they cook, grate the parmesan cheese. I use 150 gr., but feel free to use more, or less, to taste. When the zucchinis are ready, move them to the serving plate and salt them, possibly with a good salt. (I use salt flakes.)

Now drizzle them all with some extra-virgin olive oil and cover them in parmesan cheese. The zucchinis must be warm so that the heat will lightly soften the cheese. Add pepper to taste and enjoy right away.

They keep in the fridge for a day or two; just heat them up before serving. Microwave, in this case, is perfectly fine. A similar dish can be made using asparagus instead of zucchinis, and butter instead of oil.

GRILLED EGGPLANT IN MINT AND GARLIC MARINADE

FOR 6 PEOPLE

I love eggplants. I love their color, their unique flavor, and their versatility. They are delicious in a tomato sauce, stuffed, sautéed, made into meatless meatballs, and grilled, of course. This recipe is pure summer on a plate, with a fresh and Mediterranean-inspired marinade made of fresh mint leaves, extra-virgin olive oil, and garlic. This is one of my father's favorite sides and appetizers, because it can be used for either, or even in a panino. Few ingredients, lots of flavor.

Preparation: 30 minutes
Cooking time: 15-20 minutes according to the amount of eggplant
Passive time: at least 3 hours

2 eggplants
10-15 fresh mint leaves
5 cloves of garlic (whole)
Extra-virgin olive oil and salt to taste
Fresh or dry chives to taste (optional)

Rinse the eggplants and cut them crosswise, ¼-inch thick.
Place eggplants in a big pasta colander and sprinkle with abundant salt. Allow to rest for 30 minutes.

Rinse the eggplant slices and pat dry.

Grill the eggplants until lightly charred.

In a container with a lid, layer the slices of eggplant with a few mint leaves, olive oil, salt, and the clove of garlic. Continue until you have layered and dressed all the eggplant.

Close containers with the lid, gently shake, and allow to marinate for at least 2-3 hours.

Serve at room temperature as a side dish or in your favorite preparation.

You can keep these in the fridge in an airtight container for 3-4 days.
They are actually amazing the day after.

KALE AND ESCAROLE SOUP WITH LEMON, PARMESAN CHEESE, AND CANNELLINI BEANS

FOR 4 PEOPLE

I find it romantic that, when I think about my mom's cooking, all the dishes she makes for my father come to mind. I think that my mom has always cooked with my father's happiness in mind. And this dish, which is a creation of mine inspired by her, reminds me of the same thing: my father's happiness. It's so healthy and flavorful that it is truly the poster-dish for how vegetables can rock your dinner and make you completely forget meat.

Preparation: 15 minutes
Cooking time: 20 minutes

1 head of escarole
1 bunch of curly kale
2 cans of cannellini beans
1 shallot
2 cloves of garlic, whole
1 lemon (juice and zest)
4 parmesan cheese rinds
Extra-virgin olive oil, salt, and chili flakes to taste
1 pinch of coconut sugar or brown sugar

Rinse the kale and the escarole, then blanch both in salted boiling water for 5 minutes. This will get rid of some of the bitterness of the escarole and will soften the kale.

After 5 minutes, drain most of the cooking water and set aside.

In a skillet, sauté the garlic and the finely chopped shallot in extra-virgin olive oil, then add the vegetables with at least 1 full cup of their cooking water.

Simmer for 10 minutes, then add the beans.

Taste for salt and pepper, maybe add some more olive oil, and the parmesan cheese rinds Continue to simmer for a few more minutes, then add the lemon zest, the juice of half a lemon, drizzle with olive oil, and cover the skillet. Remove from the heat, remove rinds (serve them separately) and allow to rest for 10 minutes before serving.

Ideally, you would serve this with bread; place a few slices of stale or fresh bread at the bottom of a soup dish and then cover with the soup. Enjoy hot, maybe adding some chili flakes or parmesan cheese.

POTATO AND RADICCHIO GRATIN, WITH RED ONION AND PARMESAN CHEESE

FOR 2-4 PEOPLE

I decided to add this recipe in the section dedicated to my mom because, even though she hates onions, she often cooks them for my father, who loves them.

I think that my mother is one of the reasons why food and love are synonymous for me, because she cooks for my father. Even when my brother and I are there, even when we lived at home, even when she made things for us, I think that, ultimately, she made them for him.

This recipe is for 4 people when served as a side, or for 2-3 when served as the only course of the meal.

Preparation: 35 minutes
Cooking time: 15-20 minutes

4 medium yellow potatoes
1 head of radicchio
2 red onions
1 tsp. of must reduction (arrope)[11]
Extra-virgin olive oil and salt to taste
¼ cup of grated parmigiano cheese

Steam the potatoes until fully cooked but still holding texture.

Slice the red onion very thin and sauté in a generous amount of extra-virgin olive oil until soft and caramelized.

Cut the radicchio (from which you have removed the outer leaves) in 4 wedges and add it to the onion. Let it cook on every side for 5-10 minutes, then drizzle with the must reduction. Salt everything to taste and set aside.

Slice the steamed potatoes in ¼-inch rounds.

Transfer the radicchio and the onion to a 9x12 baking dish, then cover with the sliced potatoes. Drizzle with olive oil, salt to taste, and cover the surface of the potatoes with a generous amount of freshly grated parmigiano cheese.

Bake for 15-20 minutes at 350°F; allow to rest for 5 minutes before serving.

---

11 In Italian, must reduction is called "vin cotto," literally "cooked wine." It is sweet and deep in flavor, with a gentle tang that is perfect for adding to bitter ingredients. In the south of Italy, they use it often to glaze a crunchy deep-fried dough (cardellate).

FARINATA

This recipe is a traditional Italian one that dates back to generations. Originally from the region of Liguria, farinata is the ultimate Italian street food, so simple and healthy that you won't believe how good it is until you have tried a slice. At that point, this will become one of your go-to's for your family and to surprise your friends. This is one of my favorite Italian dishes, I like it even better than pizza!

This recipe makes three 12-inch round pizza pans[12] .

Preparation: 5 minutes
Passive time: 2-3 hours
Cooking time: 20-25 minutes

900 ml. (30.4 fl. oz.) of room-temperature filtered water
300 gr. (10.6 oz.) of chickpea flour
4 tbsp. (50 ml.) of extra-virgin olive oil
2 tsp. (10 gr.) of fine sea salt
1 tbsp. finely chopped rosemary leaves (optional)
Black pepper, to taste

In a big mixing bowl, stir together the water and the chickpea flour, whisk, and cover. Set aside and let the mixture rest for 2-3 hours.

After 2-3 hours remove the foam that has formed on the surface.

Add the oil and the salt and whisk.

If you want, add the rosemary.

Generously oil the 3 pans, then pour the mixture, in equal parts, with a ladle, in all 3.
Bake in a pre-heated oven to 480°F for 10 minutes, then lower to 450°F and continue baking until the farinata is a beautiful golden color. Serve hot with plenty of fresh black pepper.

---

12 Traditionally, a copper pan is used. At home, I make it with a regular non-stick pizza pan.

PEPERONATA (BELL PEPPER STEW)

FOR 6 PEOPLE

Peperonata is another Italian classic that my mom makes all the time. It is one of my favorite ways to eat bell peppers, my very favorite vegetable. This is a classic on every Italian table during the summer months, when bell peppers are ripe, juicy, and intense in flavor and color.[13] My version of this dish includes onions; my mother's does not: the result is to die for either way.

I also like to add a pinch of brown sugar to help with the acidity of the bell peppers. A perfect side dish to eggs, meats, tofu, or rice, it is a classic with oven-roasted chicken or fennel seed sausage.

The secret to a perfect peperonata is patience: this is a very simple dish that requires a slow cook, and it is absolutely worth the time.

Preparation: 15 minutes
Cooking time: 1 hour

6 bell peppers of different color
1 shallot
1 pinch of brown sugar
2-3 leaves of fresh basil
Extra-virgin olive oil to taste
Salt and pepper to taste
1 clove of garlic, whole

Cut the bell peppers in half, remove the seeds, and then cut them into 1½-inch pieces.

Finely chop the shallot and sauté in extra-virgin olive oil for a minute or two with the clove of garlic.

Remove the garlic, add the bell peppers, the basil, salt, and sugar, lower the heat to medium-low, and keep cooking, covered with a lid and stirring frequently to prevent from sticking until the bell peppers are fully cooked and very soft. This usually takes 45 minutes to an hour.

Serve warm as a side to fish or meat or eat at room temperature as an appetizer. You can add some balsamic reduction or balsamic vinegar to it as well, but I prefer mine without.

---

13 *Peak season for bell peppers is July, August, and September. You can find them year-round in the grocery stores, of course, but nothing can beat the flavor of in-season vegetables. I love to wait for summer to have this dish, as it reminds me of how food used to be when I was a child. I still respect the seasons when I cook; it makes me feel aligned with the natural way of life.*

FENNEL GRATIN
WITH BÉCHAMEL SAUCE

FOR 4 PEOPLE

This dish is one that Mom makes often, because both she and my father love fennel. I love it too, raw, sautéed, even steamed.

My version of béchamel is a little lighter than a traditional French one, and it can also be made with oat milk.

"Real" béchamel uses whole milk, while here I am using 2%. It's easy to make, and you can even freeze the leftovers.

Preparation; 15 minutes
Cooking time: 45 minutes

4 fennel bulbs
4 tbsp. (50 gr.) of unsalted butter + ½ tbsp. to butter the baking dish
500 ml. (17 fl. oz.) of 2% milk
50 gr (1.7 oz.) of all-purpose flour
1 pinch of salt
Nutmeg to taste
Extra-virgin olive oil, salt, and pepper to taste
2 tbsp. of parmigiano cheese, grated

Clean the fennel by removing the tops and the outer leaves (keep all this in a bag and freeze to make vegetable stock).

Quarter the fennel bulbs and steam in a double boiler until tender (15 minutes).

While the fennel steams, prepare the béchamel.

Heat the milk in a saucepan.

Separately, melt the butter over low heat, then turn off the heat and add the flour all at once, as if you were making pâte à Choux, Choux pastry, stirring with a whisk. Then, put the saucepan back over low heat and stir until the mixture becomes golden. This step cooks the flour for a pleasant and toasty flavor.

Infuse the milk with nutmeg and salt to taste.

Pour a little hot milk over the roux (flour and butter mixture), whisk, then slowly add the remaining milk, whisking vigorously.

Cook for 5 minutes over low heat until it starts to thicken, and you reach the desired consistency. I like to have a more liquid sauce for this recipe, so I don't cook it too much.

Butter a baking dish and arrange the fennel.

Drizzle with olive oil, salt, and pepper to taste, and then cover with as much béchamel you wish. I don't cover the entire dish with sauce because I want a lighter result, but you can cover the fennel in its entirety.

Grate some parmigiano cheese and bake for 15 minutes at 400°F.

Let the dish rest for a few minutes before serving.

SAUTÉED CARROTS WITH ROSEMARY AND CINNAMON

FOR 4 PEOPLE

wrote this story in 2015 for a tentative food memoir I was working on, before this book came along. Catherine hadn't been born yet, and Ben and I were just married.

This isn't fiction. I decided to add it to this book, even though the writing may sound different from the rest of the short essays you have read so far, because without this event I wouldn't be cooking.

The simple recipe that follows is the dish I was making when I finally realized I needed help to break the chains of unhealthy patterns that didn't serve me anymore, and that were ruining my life and my marriage.

Ben and I still lived in Tarzana. One quiet evening in March 2015, I came home from Whole Foods and, like almost every night, I began to make dinner.

Picture a beautiful kitchen with stainless steel countertops, white cabinets, and hard-wood floors. Behind the sink that opens up on the wooden breakfast counter there are two bamboo stems in narrow vases of clear glass half-filled with fresh water; natural light filters through them, and the reflection brightens up the room.

I look at the clock over the little radio that we keep by the sink; it is 45 minutes after five, and on KPCC[14] "All Things Considered" is halfway in. With striking punctuality, Ben parks his car and enters the kitchen through the garage.

"Hey babe, I missed you." He smiles and kisses me.

He is wearing a Paul Smith long-sleeve purple shirt over black jeans, and he looks sharp, elegant, timeless. On his right hand, a silver ring sparkles, and so does the David Yurman dark green stone at his neck, with matching cufflinks, that we have bought together in Chicago the year before. He looks like a rock star in disguise.

I am in black leggings and an old, pale blue sweatshirt; I am not wearing any make up, and my hair is tied in a long braid. I look at him, picture-perfect with his two-day beard and his silver hair, prince charming; I feel like Cinderella before the little glass slipper.

"I'm making sautéed carrots with rosemary," I say, feeling jittery, even though the day has been quite uneventful. Nothing bad happened, it was a normal day. I am just anxious.

"Oh, great, I love it!" Ben is always happy when I cook. And dinner is the most important meal of the day for us. While I'm cooking, he sets the table. We don't have a television in the kitchen, so he puts a record on, Julie London, *How Deep Is The Ocean*.

"Thank you for dinner, chef," he always says with a kiss. And as we eat, we talk about our day, about something we have read in the paper, or about a new book we ought to get; sometimes we discuss our future plans. We are newly married, and we are very much in love.

After dinner, we clear the table together, we wash the dishes, and we make ginger tea for me, and peppermint for him.

Ben pays attention to the details, he always asks about the ingredients and the preparation of a dish, and after glimpsing with curiosity at the food on the kitchen counter, almost taking mental note of what he is about to eat, he puts his car keys away and heads to the bedroom.

I am alone in the room now, and from the sink, where I stand washing my hands, I see the pool garden and the beautiful view over the San Fernando Valley.

At the store, I have bought Italian extra-virgin olive oil, a head of garlic, and organic carrots. The rosemary I have picked from the garden. The wooden stem deposits some resin on my hands, and as I mince it on my new wooden cutting board, I inhale deeply its earthy, wintry and intense aroma. Rosemary reminds me of mountain air, of simple lives, of my Italian roots.

And speaking of roots, carrots are my favorite vegetable to munch on before dinner; their bright color is inviting, and the texture is harmoniously layered from the very outer peel to the heart, spiny and milder in taste.

I linger on their color because, only a few weeks earlier, I had stumbled upon a reading about carrots, a vegetable that, originally, was purple and yellow, and mainly found in Afghanistan and vicinity—far from where my roots are, the Alps, and yet so very reminiscent of home. Their growth circles are similar to a tree's, and they change in tonality of orange, from very bright to pale, and then bright again, at the very center.

I eat a carrot layer by layer, from the outer one to the heart, like I did when I was a child.

I feel less anxious, focusing on the food helped me relax, but the calm doesn't last for long.

It's 6:30 now, and it's getting late. On KPCC, "Market Place" has just begun. I don't have a ticking clock to dinnertime, but I feel rushed.

"We should watch Fred and Ginger," Ben says, walking back into the kitchen to watch me cook. He sounds happy, looking forward to spending a quiet night at home watching old movies.

"Sure, babe," I say. I am not in the present, neither in the conversation with him or in the preparation of dinner.

For some reason I am still trying to understand, I am afraid of intimacy, so when something intimate is about to happen, like dinner and a movie, which I consider intimate, I subconsciously tend to find ways to detach from the present: I create a buffer between me and the person, the moment, and the feeling, so that I can run away, instigate a fight, hide.

I set aside the minced rosemary, and I finally begin to prepare the carrots. I cut their leafy ends, and with a ceramic peeler, I remove the thin outer layer. I notice the bright red of the peeler's handle that, with the orange of the carrots, reflects harmoniously into the stainless steel of the countertops. For a second I recapture the relaxed mood of just a few minutes before.

Once the carrots are clean, I grab the box grater that I have bought the year before, when I still lived by myself in a cozy and "rustic" one-bedroom apartment on the Hollywood Hills.

---

14 KPCC is our local NPR radio that is always on, in the kitchen

I never spent much time in its tiny kitchenette. The narrow, rectangular open space was somber. I had thoroughly cleaned the kitchen cabinets when I had moved in, in 2012, but they had been painted with a shade of brown that resembled mud more than chocolate. They were made of wood, but their paint had chipped, and I could easily smell their history. Very different from my new kitchen, the old one felt even smaller than it actually was, because of its dark green walls, and because of the old, stained linoleum floor.

When Ben and I had gotten married, a few weeks earlier, I had brought some of my kitchen utensils to the new house. I felt a sense of pride for contributing something that was mine, in a home that had everything I could wish for, but that had been presented to me emotionally furnished, previously inhabited by an ex-wife and an ex-girlfriend, but never inspired by the union of our hearts, taste, and dreams.

When I look at the clock it's already 6:45, so I begin to slice the first carrot—as thin as possible so that it can stay crunchy and slightly burned along the edges, just the way my mother cooked them, when I was a child.

I notice that the grater has lost sharpness, and I worry because I have half-pound of carrots to slice; nothing else would cut them thin enough within a reasonable time. But worry soon turns into irritation. The skin around my mouth begins to itch, an early and uncomfortable sign that always precedes an episode. The feeling of discomfort and enmity starts in my brain, but it swiftly becomes physical as well. My marvel at the composition of a carrot has vanished.

I can't believe that there isn't a real mandolin, I think.

I grow increasingly irritated by how the preparation of my dinner is proceeding. Ben is scrolling through his phone, but he is also looking at me, fascinated by how I seem to look confident wearing the apron he has gotten me. This, to me, starts to feel intimate.

I try to focus on the cool temperature of the hardwood floor under my feet, but it is in the greenery that surrounds the house in which I seem to find temporary solace. I refrain from complaining, or losing my temper, but just as I have feared and predicted—due to the occurrence of similar episodes in the past—after a quick glimpse at the palm trees in the garden I turn blind. I can only focus on the broken multi-purpose box grater that I still hold in my right hand.

I turn my back to Ben, and that's when I lose control. It happens quickly, and so violently that I can barely perceive the split.

"Fuck!" I yell, smashing the grater on the floor.

I have cut my finger trying to slice the carrot, and the blade that had seemed to not be working on the vegetables has proved to be sharp enough to cut through my skin just fine.

"I can help you with the carrots, babe. It's not a big deal." Ben tries to calm me down.

But the uncomfortable itch that I have started feeling around my mouth a few minutes before, and that I have tried to suppress, now escapes its restraints and turns to rage. If just a few seconds earlier I hadn't been able to see past the sink and through the adjacent room, after I have cut myself, I can't see past the blades that—in my head—have turned against me.

Deaf to anything other than anger I let "the other voice in my head" take over. *She* takes charge from that moment on; my lucid self succumbs. My alter ego, the other voice, that is, feels resentful, and it's full of hatred.

I deserve this, my thought is.

"See? Nothing works in my life," I say to Ben, who looks at me, saddened and preoccupied; this isn't the first time he has witnessed his wife falling apart.

"I'm done with this, Ben. I swear!" Not entirely sure what I am done with, I take my frustration out on him, precisely what I had tried to avoid a few minutes before.

I can't pause and I can't see a solution. Things happen quickly when I am angry, and it's very difficult to stop them without feeling weak, and like a loser. I see a war that doesn't exist; powerless otherwise, I hold onto my self-righteous thoughts to feel in charge, and to fight back. Rationally, I know that I am fighting ghosts, but nothing's rational when I am angry.

I hear two voices in my head: The angry one that has been silent for a while needs to take charge and feel powerful by starting a fight; the other knows where anger takes me, but it's fearful and tired.

When these episodes of uncontrolled anger occur, I feel possessed, and I become aggressive. I lose control over my impulses and I regress to when I was five years old; I verbally attack my loved ones, I hit myself, too, and the objects around me. Like a child, I break them, because my ego sees them as enemies. Then, after an indefinite amount of time—exhausted and deprived of most of my vital force—the other voice leaves my head, and the alter ego leaves my body. It is at this point that I am left worn out, emptied, and ashamed.

The broken carrot grater wasn't the problem.

Devastated, I let myself fall heavy on the kitchen floor, and I cry the tears that I have tried to suppress before. My finger is bleeding, but I don't feel pain. I observe the little stream of blood and I lick my finger; I keep it in my mouth for a few seconds, and then I look at more blood come out. With my fist I hit my thighs, and then I hit the floor. I hit the kitchen cabinets and scream: "Leave me alone, okay?" But Ben has left the room. "Dinner is ruined!" I dramatically announce.

I tuck my knees to my chest and approach an almost catatonic state. My muscles are so rigid that I can barely move; I am frozen in that moment of loss and chaos.

With my fists clenched I keep my body grounded and the tension high. I want to scream, but I seem to have lost my voice. So, I scream inside, and the sound I produce bounces within the bones of my chest; it echoes back to my head, making chaos even more unmanageable. When I'm angry, I can't discern every word that I utter in my head, but when I calm down every sound is amplified in both meaning and volume. I remember the voice of sanity, but never my ego's, in flame.

I feel so alone!

I need to be hugged and reassured, but when Ben tried to hold me, I had pushed him away and turned him into my enemy. The pain I have caused him hurts me more than my own.

I want not to care so much. I want to take things more lightly. I want to feel normal.

When an anger episode subsides, my brain perceives acts such as reaching out, asking for help, or making amends, as signs of weakness and defeat. So, the return to a state of normality happens very slowly. It can take entire days for the "the good voice" to be in charge of me again.

Now that I am calmer, I wonder where Ben is, and yet I am too ashamed to call him.

"Babe," I whisper in my head. "Help me, please." I have a terrible headache.

But Ben isn't far at all. He has never really left. "Alice, please," he calmly says as he walks back to the kitchen to make sure that I am okay. "Ask for help, my love." My muscles have begun to relax, and both my hands rest on my thighs. I am still on the floor.

His eyes don't show pity, but unconditional love. In that moment, his eyes try to tell me a story I have never heard before, and with love and tenderness they dry mine, in tears. Ben's eyes are transparent—they cannot lie.

He didn't deserve my darkness, and neither did I. I knew that I had to break the chain and understand why I held so much anger inside. I knew that if I hadn't listened to him our marriage would be in danger, and that I would be, too.

So, a couple of days after the evening in March when I cooked roasted carrots for supper, I called Dr. W.

I was finally ready to heal, and it had all begun in the kitchen.

Preparation: 20 minutes
Cooking time: 40-45 minutes

1½ pound of carrots
2 stems of fresh rosemary, either whole or minced
2 cloves of garlic (whole)
1 pinch of ground cinnamon
4-5 tbsp. of extra-virgin olive oil
Freshly ground black pepper, to taste
Sea salt, to taste

Rinse and finely mince the rosemary. Set aside.

Now rinse and peel the carrots, and in a mixing bowl, thinly slice them with a mandolin (or in the food processor). I like to keep a round/oval shape. Set aside.

In a 12-inch non-stick frying pan or skillet, heat the extra virgin olive oil with the whole cloves of garlic, and after a minute or two, throw the carrots in; stir and add the rosemary.

Sauté until carrots are soft, almost caramelized, and slightly charred along the edges (approximately 45 minutes). Stir regularly. Add salt, cinnamon, and pepper to taste.

Remove garlic and serve warm.

I wrote the following essay in 2017, when I was on what turned out to be the last tour of Tom Petty and the Heartbreakers. I decided to write an introduction to an essay as if it were a recipe, because looking back at those days, I can see all the ingredients that made this book.

I was pregnant during the tour; I was often sick, because the tour started when I was 4 weeks and heavily affected by "morning sickness." I remember Dallas and New Orleans being very difficult; I remember being scared, but also excited. Being the spring of 2017, nobody had any idea that only a few months later, death and birth would walk hand in hand.

Sometimes I wish I had known, because I believe my relationship with my pregnant body would have been different.

Would we behave differently if we knew we were about to die or someone we love would?

Would have I worried as much about the weight I was gaining, had I known that Tom would not live to meet my daughter?

I don't know.

I do know that when I read this essay, and when I read the essay dedicated to Tom, I am reminded of how much my disease and my self-obsession detach me from reality, from the beauty and the intensity of reality, good and bad, happy or sad.

One of the reasons I have decided to include these essays in my cookbook is that I will use this book for my own daily cooking, and I need to be reminded of all the events, the ingredients, and the instruction that brought me to the life I have today. Not a perfect one—one in which I often make mistakes, and in which I don't always gracefully deal with difficulties, but one in which I am aware and willing to heal, to move forward, to share the journey, and to never, never, never give up.

THANK YOU, TOM

from 2017

"Will you still be my mom in heaven?" I'd ask my mom when I was a little girl. We lived in a very small apartment, and my feelings were so overwhelmingly big that they had never quite fit.

"Do you think we'll still be married after we die?" I asked Ben a while back.

I was reading about black holes in the *New York Times*, and I started to cry thinking about the end of all things. "Why are we even trying to have a child? What if we forget about each other in whatever other life there is out there? What if nothing happens after we die?" I panicked and, in tears, curled smaller and smaller in his arms.

Since my early childhood, I recall being taken over by a constant and devastating sense of fear of the end, whether of a game, a vacation, an experience, a job, a relationship, a situation—and ultimately, the end of life.

I have never really been concerned with missing the object of change, the person, or the situation, but rather with the aftermath, with change itself, with the divide between now and tomorrow.

This preoccupation haunted my everyday life until I closed my eyes on it through the abuse of food, drugs, and alcohol. I never walked through the woods; I never worked it out.

So inevitably, when I got sober, in 2012, I was little Alice all over again, heartbroken every time I had to say goodbye, turn a page, close a book.

Life went on; I got better at dealing with it. And yet my attachment to the present and my defiance in the face of change stayed the same: when I fell in love and married Ben, I began to live in fear of life without him. With the countless blessings in our life the fear of tragedy came, with financial bounty the terror of poverty, and with health the dread of sickness, loneliness, and death.

Since Tom passed on Monday night, all those fears gathered up and thundered in my head in unison: what would happen now?

"He is the first close person in my life that has passed away in my adulthood and sobriety," I told Ben the following morning as we lay in bed holding each other, after the previous 24 hours of pain, shock, and disbelief, but also of family and love.

In fact, the closest people in my life that had left this world had been my maternal grandparents, who died when I was 19 and 23 (years when I wasn't exactly "all there").

As I was writing this piece, I looked back and saw how things have ended, yes, but then begun, time and time again. Life has so far known exactly how to write its own book. My fears neither hinder nor prevent what had to come, whether good or bad. Life always continued to happen.

In the wake of death, it is in the experience of life that I seem to find some hope, some kind strength. And I don't have to look back to find it: it is the new life that I am growing inside that is guiding me toward the acceptance of change, birth, and death, old and new, beginnings and endings.

I can fear all that, or I can feel all that.

"Can't you see that it's not up to us?"

I said that to Ben once we had gotten up and decided to start the day, a difficult one. I felt discouraged and powerless.

He had just told me that he is doing everything he can to be with us forever—for he knows me well—he knows what's inside my heart.

And it is true: when we live, or when we die, is not up to us. But we choose how to live until we die.

In dealing with grief, I want to be fearless today. I want to tell little Alice, the me that is still afraid, that she can say goodbye without being heartbroken; she can close a book and open a new one, because the stories she has already read will never go away. This is also what I want to teach our daughter. For what inevitably passes never truly leaves us: it gives us fertile soil to plant anew, to begin again, and again, and again.

On Monday night, at the hospital, our baby girl moved in my womb more than ever before, almost as if to let us know she was part of what was happening; I could touch her little foot (or elbow?) pressing against my skin.

I introduced her to Tom. Ben was devastated at the thought his brother-in-song would never meet his daughter. I felt the deepest connection, and some who were present seemed to feel the same—life and death together as one, a reminder of what our existence is: ephemeral, precious in its fragility. So, with sorrow in my heart, today, but not with a broken heart, I choose to see the gift instead of the punishment, the gain instead of the loss. And if this is what I learned from Tom's new beginning, I can only say:

"Thank you, Tom."

CAKES, TARTS, AND PUDDINGS

PISTACHIO AND ORANGE BLOSSOM SBRISOLONA (CRUMBLE CAKE)

FOR 6-8 PEOPLE

Sbrisolona is a traditional crumbly cake from Mantova, Italy. The name comes from the dialect word *brìsa*, which means *briciola* in Italian, crumb. The classic recipe is made of just almonds, rigorously with the peel on, but I wanted to play on my love for pistachios and orange blossom and create a marriage of cultures, Persian and Italian. I love this cake because it's buttery and messy, not quite a cake, not quite a cookie, it is full of texture, so when you eat it, you keep munching on it, crumb after crumb, as if it were a bag of chips.

Preparation: 15 minutes
Cooking time: 40 minutes

200 gr. (7 oz. or approximately 1½ cup) of fine polenta
200 gr. (7 oz. or approximately 1½ cup) of all-purpose flour
7 tbsp. (100 gr.) unsalted butter at room temperature
200 gr. (7 oz.) shelled, unsalted raw pistachios
120 gr. (4.2 oz. or approximately ½ cup) of cane sugar
2 egg yolks
A few drops of orange blossom extract (*a little goes a long way*)
A generous pinch of salt
Zest of 1 orange

Pre-heat oven to 375°F.

Coarsely chop the unsalted pistachios.

In a mixing bowl, combine all the dry ingredients, including the pistachios and the orange zest. Create a well in the middle and add the egg yolk, the orange blossom, and the butter, soft at room temperature.

Mix with your hands until the batter comes together in the form of big crumbs.

Butter a round cake tin with detachable bottom and transfer the batter in it. With a fork, level the cake without pressing the dough.

Bake for 40 minutes and allow to completely cool down before removing from the tin.
Transfer to a serving plate and freely break the cake into crumbs.

SALTED CARAMEL & CITRUS UPSIDE-DOWN CAKE

FOR 6-8 PEOPLE

I made this cake when I became increasingly interested with Buddha's Hand. I had seen pictures of it in food magazines before, but one day, during the pandemic, I bought it at the farmers' market. I think that, in the pandemic, I felt so isolated that trying new flavors and ingredients made me feel as if I were traveling, eating out with friends, discovering new dishes…

I fell in love with Buddha's Hand at the first bite. The farmer had told me to try it raw first, slice a piece and eat it, without sugar, or condiments: I couldn't believe how delicate it was, how sweet, how good. Crunchy with a soft heart, a mild lemon without juice or seeds, but infused with vanilla, so elegant and subtle that I began to cook it in every possible way, even grilled and baked with oil, salt, and rosemary. I added it to my crackers, to cookies, and to cakes like the one you are about to make.

This is the perfect winter cake to have for tea, as a decadent dessert at night without guilt (it's a pretty light and healthy cake), or for breakfast. Because nothing like a beautiful cake helps start the day with the right foot.

Preparation: 20 minutes
Passive time 30 minutes + 1 hour
Cooking time: 60-65 minutes

For the cake:

260 gr. (9.2 oz. or approximately 2⅛ cup) of all-purpose flour
100 gr. (3.5 oz. or approximately ½ cup) of caster sugar
Zest of 1 orange and 1 lemon
2 tbsp. (35 gr. or 1.2 oz.) of finely chopped Buddha's Hand
    (or the zest of an extra lemon if you don't have it)
2 eggs at room temperature
6 tbsp. (85 gr.) of unsalted butter, softened at room temperature
¼ tsp. baking soda
2.4 tsp. (10 gr.) of baking powder
1 tsp. vanilla paste
250 gr. (8.8 oz. or approximately 1 cup) of whole milk plain yogurt
    (at room temperature)
Any leftover juice from the bowl of the oranges for the topping.

For the salted caramel:

130 gr. (4.6 oz.) of sugar
¼ tsp. salt (or to taste)
3½ tbsp. (45 gr.) of butter
1 tbsp. half and half

For the topping:

>2 oranges finely sliced (*I used blood oranges*)
>1 tsp. brown sugar

Pre-heat oven to 325°F.

In a small mixing bowl, slice the oranges finely and coat them in some sugar and grapefruit zest. Butter an 8-inch round cake pan and place a layer of parchment paper at the bottom. Butter the parchment paper also, and when ready, assemble the finely sliced oranges in a neat circle (remember this will be the top of your cake). Set aside and start working on the caramel.

Caramel is always tricky, but the good thing is that this time, we don't really care if it comes out a little grainy; actually, this is more of a toffee, a salted one. In a small saucepan, melt butter and sugar and salt to taste (I like this salty) until the butter melts completely; try not to stir too much, just enough to prevent the sugar from burning and the mix to blend. As soon as it starts to boil, add the half and half, and let it darken until it resembles a light toffee (approximately 5 minutes from boiling). If it thickens too much, you can always add a little bit more half and half.

Remove from heat and delicately pour over the oranges. Set aside and allow to cool. Do not spread it with a fork; it will make a mess. It doesn't have to cover the oranges perfectly.
Make sure all your ingredients are at room temperature and that the butter has softened at room temperature.

In the bowl of a stand mixer, combine all the dry ingredients and the zest of orange and lemon. If you are using the Buddha's Hand (highly recommended), chop it finely and add it to the dry ingredients. Set aside.

In a small mixing bowl, lightly beat the eggs, any remaining juice from the sliced oranges, the yogurt, and the vanilla paste. Sometimes, I like to add 10 ml. of rum.
With the paddle attachment, mix the dry ingredients and the softened butter until it becomes sandy, and the butter disappears.

Add the egg mixture and continue to mix at medium speed for 1 minute until all the ingredients are nicely incorporated. Do not over-mix.

Pour the batter onto the cake pan, over the oranges and caramel, level the cake with a spatula, and remove any air bubbles by tapping the cake pan on the countertop (perhaps over a towel, if you have delicate countertop like mine). This batter is very thick because of the yogurt, don't worry, it will be spectacular.

Bake the cake at 325°F until well risen and nicely golden (approximately 60-65 minutes). A toothpick will come out dry and clean when the cake is ready.

Let the cake rest in the pan for 30 minutes before flipping it. Help yourself by making sure, with a knife, that all the sides have detached from the pan, then flip the cake onto the serving plate. Delicately remove the parchment paper from the top of the cake and allow to rest for at least an hour before serving.

AMARETTO TIRAMISU

FOR 6–8 PEOPLE

Tiramisu is one of my favorite desserts. One day I decided to make it on the show but realized, too late, that I had run out of ladyfingers. Something I always have in my pantry, however, is amaretti cookies. They are light and healthy when I crave something sweet (they are amazing just crumbled in yogurt, or on ice cream). So, I decided to use them, and this dessert ended up in the book.

Preparation: 45 minutes
Passive time: at least 2 hours

300 ml. (10-11 fl. oz.) of espresso
  (*Use a good coffee, possibly brewed on the stove with an Italian mocha.*)
500 gr. (17.5 oz.) of mascarpone cheese
350 gr. amaretti cookies (12.5 oz.) + 50 gr. (1.5 oz.) of ladyfingers
  (*I like to mix the two. You may use less than the amount suggested,*
  but I like a tiramisu nicely loaded with all the goodness.)
4 fresh eggs
80 gr. (2.8 oz.) caster sugar
4 tbsp. raw unsweetened cocoa powder
2 tsp. (10 ml.) rum extract or marsala wine (optional)

Make the coffee ahead, so it's not hot when we dip the cookies. I highly suggest a quality, strong espresso. I don't like sweet coffee, so I did not add any sugar, but you can. Just be remember the cream and the cookies are sweet.

Separate the yolks from the whites. Make sure there is no trace of yolk in the whites, or they will not beat to peak. Also, wash your hands after breaking the eggs so as not to contaminate the food.

In a mixing bowl, start beating the yolks and 30 gr. of sugar with a hand mixer.
When it starts to be a little lighter and fluffier, prepare the simple syrup to pasteurize the yolks. In a small saucepan, mix 25 ml. of water with 20 gr. of sugar. Bring to a boil and cook until it reaches 250°F. You will need a thermometer for this, because after 250°F the sugar will caramelize, and we want it liquid but hot enough to pasteurize the eggs.

Now keep beating the yolks and the sugar while adding the hot syrup. Your eggs are pasteurized. Keep beating until light in color and fluffy, then set aside.

Now, in a separate mixing bowl, whip the mascarpone, and add a couple of tablespoons of yolk mixture to start making the cream. Now fold in the remaining egg mixture and use a hand mixer to create a smooth cream. Set aside.

Now let's beat the egg whites with 10 gr. of sugar until we reach stiff peaks.

In the same small saucepan, prepare the same syrup to pasteurize the whites. Same as before, 25 ml. of water to 20 gr. of sugar. When the syrup reaches 250°F, let's beat the whites more while adding the syrup.

If you flip the bowl with your egg whites and nothing moves or falls, it means you have reached the desired consistency. So now fold into the whites 2 tablespoons of the yolk-cheese mixture. Then, very gently fold the whites in the big yolk mixture, from bottom to top.

Choose your serving dish, and let's assemble the dessert: layer some cream at the bottom, then dip the amaretti in coffee for 2 seconds and build a layer of cookies. Now cover the cookies with more cream, dust with cocoa powder and repeat until you have used all the cream. Alternate amaretti and lady fingers. Finish with cocoa powder.

Allow to rest in the fridge for at least 2 hours before serving. The day after it will be even better.

Note: If you drink alcohol, add some marsala wine or rum extract to the cream and it will make it truly special. You can use decaf coffee if you want.

GREEK YOGURT AND CHIA SEEDS TRIFLE, WITH RUM AND MIXED FRUIT

FOR 4 PORTIONS

As you have probably understood, I love my dessert after every meal. As you also have probably understood, I care about healthy food—comfort food that is also healthy, that is.

This trifle perfectly embodies all the above: decadent, creamy, boozy, fresh, fruity, healthy.

It's extremely easy to make, very quick, and best if done the night before, so that the ladyfingers can soak up all the goodness of both rum and fruit.

If you want this sweeter, feel free to add more sugar, and play with the fruit you have, whether frozen or fresh.

Preparation: 35-40 minutes
Passive time: at least 3 hours, even better overnight

350 gr. (12.3 oz. approximately 1½ cup) full-fat Greek yogurt
3 tbsp. (45 gr.) chia seeds
3 or 3½ tbsp. (50 gr.) maple syrup + 1 tbsp. for the fruit
200 gr. (7 oz. or approximately 1½ cup) of your favorite fruit, either fresh or frozen.
(I like to mix both, as I always end up with leftovers of frozen berries and mango in the freezer. I like to add 1 kiwi, the juice of ½ an orange and the zest of 1 orange. You can add lemon zest, the orange itself, papaya, raspberries, mandarin, kumquats, pretty much anything juicy.)
1 tsp. of rum or ¼ tsp. of rum extract (I don't drink, so I go for the extract)
1 tsp. of honey (optional, for the fruit)
10-15 ladyfingers
1 tsp. of vanilla paste
1 or 2 tbsp. of almond milk or regular milk
homemade whipped cream *(optional but recommended)*

In a mixing bowl, stir together yogurt, almond milk, maple syrup, chia seeds, and vanilla paste. Mix well and set aside. The chia seeds will transform the mix into a beautiful custard.

Now prepare the fruit mix in another bowl; chop the fruit bite-size, thawing the frozen one, if using it. Make sure to keep all the juice in. Add the remaining sugar and the honey, the rum, the orange juice, and zest, and set it aside for 5-10 minutes.

Choose 4 jars of your choice and start layering the trifle: begin with a layer of fruit, then the ladyfingers (if using small jars, like I do, cut the cookie to the preferred size for layering so that it fits the jar). You can also make this in one big pretty bowl, rather than in single portion jars. If you do, you can use the ladyfingers whole.

Add some of the juice of the fruit and more fruit before adding the yogurt custard layer. Repeat, and end the dessert with a thick, generous layer of custard.

Transfer to the fridge and wait at least 3 hours before serving. I like to make this one day ahead; the cookies will soak up all the goodness and all the flavors will come together much more nicely after spending the night.

PUFFED RICE CAKE WITH NOT-SO-SWEET PASTRY CREAM

FOR 8 PEOPLE

This cake is so simple and yet so sophisticated. It's the perfect bite for an afternoon tea in the garden. The ingredients aren't many, and the preparation is easy and fun.

Preparation: 15 minutes
Cooking time: 30-35 minutes for the cake, 10 minutes for the pastry cream
Passive time: 1 hour

For the pastry cream:

700 ml. (23.7 fl. oz.) of whole or 2% milk
1 vanilla bean
1 lemon (peel only)
85 gr. (2.9 oz) of sugar
4 egg yolks
50 gr. (1.7 oz.) of potato or corn starch

For the cake:

200 gr. (7 oz. or approximately 1½ cup) of all-purpose flour
35 gr. (1.2 oz. or approximately ⅓ cup) of unsweetened puffed rice
100 gr. (3.5 oz. or approximately 7 tbsp.) of butter at room temperature
120 gr. (4.2 oz.) of sugar
1 tsp. (5 gr.) of baking powder
1 pinch of salt
1½ tsp. vanilla extract
150 ml. (5 fl. oz.) of buttermilk at room temperature
3 eggs at room temperature
1 pinch of baking soda
Zest of one lemon

For the pastry cream:

Pour milk into a saucepan with the vanilla bean (both bean and stick) and the peel of the lemon. Peel the lemon with a carrot peeler and add the peel whole. We'll remove it later. Bring milk to a light simmer without boiling.

In a mixing bowl, whisk together egg yolks, sugar, and starch.

When the milk is ready, remove the vanilla bean and the lemon peels, then slowly pour into the egg mixture in 3 parts. Do this very gently and slowly and always mixing so not to curdle the eggs.

Now pour the mixture back in the saucepan at a very low heat and cook until it has become smooth and dense enough to fill a cake. It's very important to always whisk the mixture so it doesn't curdle and stick to the bottom.

When it's ready, approximately 5 minutes, pour the pastry cream into a bowl and cover with plastic wrap, making sure the wrap is in full contact with the surface of the cream. This will prevent a layer from forming on the surface. Allow to cool down and then refrigerate.

For the cake:

Pre-heat oven to 375°F.

Butter a round 9-inch cake tin, then place parchment paper to the bottom and butter that also. I am not a fan of cooking sprays.

In a mixing bowl, cream the butter and the sugar until it forms a smooth cream. Then add the vanilla, the lemon zest, and the eggs, one at a time, incorporating each one before adding the rest. Make sure all your ingredients are at room temperature. After the eggs, add the buttermilk.

Sift through the flour, the baking powder, baking soda, and salt, then add to the wet mix.

Lastly, add the puffed rice.

Mix the dough just enough for all the ingredients to be incorporated; do not overmix.
Pour the batter into the tin and level it with a fork.

Bake for 30-35 minutes, until a toothpick comes out dry.

Leave the cake in the tin for 10 minutes before cooling down on a rack.

Allow to completely cool down before cutting.

When the cake has cooled down, delicately cut it in a half, horizontally, and spread all the pastry cream uniformly, and then re-assemble the cake.

Make sure both the cake and the pastry cream have completely cooled down before assembling the dessert. Finish the cake with a light dusting of powdered sugar.

ALMOND SOURDOUGH GALETTE WITH BERRIES

FOR 6 PEOPLE

This sourdough galette is one of my favorite ways of using leftover sourdough starter. It's also one of my favorite desserts. Easy, bright, summery, absolutely divine. It's not something that my grandmother ever made, and yet because we used to pick cherries together when I was little, at every bite I go back to Pina and Mariuccia, two cousins of my grandfather's, with whom we'd spend afternoons gathering apples, cherries, and plums. They had a very big orchard not far from where we lived, and we would go there almost every week to pick fresh fruit.

The reward of coming home and eating the hard work of the afternoon was special, something that—I believe—indirectly set the roots of my respect for where food comes from. I began to experiment with sourdough during the Covid-19 lockdown; I had gotten tired of wasting so much starter every day, so I decided to make recipes where I could substitute water, or the liquid element, with sourdough starter. In this case, I don't think I will ever go back to making this galette without it.

Preparation: 20 minutes
Cooking time: 35-40 minutes
Passive time: 30 minutes for the dough to rest in the fridge

Ingredients for the dough:

250 gr. (7 oz.) all-purpose flour
140 gr. (4.9 oz.) ripe sourdough starter (chilled)
1 stick unsalted butter, cold
¼ tsp. of salt
1 tbsp. granulated sugar (if making a sweet crust)
1 splash of iced water (if needed)
1 egg for the egg wash

Ingredients for the filling:

1½ cup mixed fresh berries
    (I used mulberries, raspberries, blueberries, and pitted cherries)
1½ tbsp. almond flour
1 tbsp. granulated sugar (or less), or 1 teaspoon of honey
½ lemon or orange juice and zest (optional)
¼ tsp. vanilla extract
almond extract

Making the dough:

In a food processor, pulse flour, salt, and cold butter (cubed) until it crumbles.

Add the chilled sourdough starter and the iced water and pulse until the mix comes together. it does so in no time, and it's important not to overwork the dough.

Pour the mix onto a pastry board and work together quickly to form a disk. Work the dough until it all comes together, form a disk, and cover in plastic wrap.

Chill the dough in the fridge for at least an hour; you can make this dough in advance and chill overnight before using it. You can freeze the dough for up to 3 months. If you do freeze it, thaw it in the fridge overnight before use.

Making the filling:

In a mixing bowl, mix your rinsed berries (cut mulberries in half and pit cherries if using them). Squeeze the juice of half a lemon (or orange), add sugar, almond flour, almond, and vanilla extracts, and stir.

Take the dough out of the fridge and roll it out in a circular shape on a lightly floured surface. Transfer to a baking sheet (this made a 15-inch pie) and don't worry about the imperfect edges. Pour filling on the dough, spread it, and then concentrate it back in the center.

Fold the edges over and pinch them to seal the pie.

With a brush, brush the crust with the beaten egg, and then sprinkle some granulated sugar. Bake at 400°F for 35-40 minutes or until the dough is nicely golden brown and the filling bubbly. Allow to cool down for 5-10 minutes and enjoy.

I also made a beautiful version of this dessert with plums, nectarines, rosemary, and orange zest. Substitute the berries with 2 small nectarines, 1-2 plums, 1 small/medium spring of rosemary, and the zest of one orange. You can also add a splash of red wine, and even a few pieces of orange, if you want. Have fun personalizing this one with your favorite fruit. In the winter, apples and pear will be fantastic, or for a more "tropical" version, go all the way with pineapple and coconut.

BLUEBERRY LEMON CRUMBLE WITH FRESH CARDAMOM

FOR 6 PEOPLE

This fresh dessert is one of my favorites in the entire book. There is something about it, perhaps the lemon zest, that makes it taste like cake batter, and the fresh cardamom gives it a beautiful intensity. The crumble is both sweet and salty, lemony, and aromatic. The blueberries are fresh and tart, and the explosion of lemon at every bite makes this pudding at once rustic and sophisticated. Easy to make, it's the perfect last-minute trick to surprise your guests after a sumptuous dinner, or yourself, at the end of a long day. Catherine loves it for breakfast.

Preparation: 15 minutes
Cooking time: 40-45 minutes

18 oz. organic blueberries
3 big lemons
90-95 gr. (3 or 3.3 oz.) of brown sugar
      (10 gr. or 2.4 tsp. for the filling, the rest for the crust)
7-10 cardamom pods
1 tsp. vanilla paste
1 generous pinch of salt
75 gr. (2.64 oz.) all-purpose flour
75 gr. (2.64 oz.) old-fashioned rolled oats
50 gr. (1.8 oz.) raw, unsalted walnuts
7 tbsp. (100 gr.) of unsalted butter, cold

Pre-heat oven to 375°F.

Take out the seeds from the cardamom pods and grind them to a powder with mortar and pestle. If you can't find the pods, you can use powdered cardamom to taste (a little goes a long way). Butter a 9x13-inch baking dish and set aside.

Rinse the blueberries, then transfer to a mixing bowl and add 10 gr. of sugar, some of the ground cardamom, the vanilla, the juice of half a lemon, and the zest of 2 lemons. Stir and pour into the buttered baking dish.

Put the flour, oats, walnuts, remaining cardamom, salt, zest of 1 lemon, and the cold butter (cut into small pieces) into a food processor, then pulse until the mixture clumps up; this usually takes a minute.

Distribute the crumble evenly over the blueberries and bake until the filling is bubbly and the crust nice and golden. This usually takes between 40 and 45 minutes.

I love to eat this crumble without the addition of ice cream or whipped cream, but feel free to serve it in combinations with either. If possible, use fresh blueberries and fresh cardamom from pods.

PEAR AND CHOCOLATE GALETTE IN CARAMELIZED SESAME CRUST

FOR 6 PEOPLE

This is one more idea for a sweet galette; as you can see, once you master the dough, the sky is the limit. Experiment with your favorite seasonal veggies and fruits, experiment with nuts to add extra flavor to the crust and have fun with decorations and toppings.

Preparation: 20 minutes
Cooking time: 35-40 minutes
Passive time: 30 minutes for the dough to rest in the fridge

Ingredients for the dough:

250 gr. (7 oz.) all-purpose flour
140 gr. (4.9 oz.) ripe sourdough starter (chilled)
1 stick unsalted butter, cold
¼ tsp. of salt
1 tbsp. granulated sugar (if making a sweet crust)
1 splash of iced water (if needed)
1 egg for the egg wash

Ingredients for the filling:

2 pears
1 tsp. vanilla paste
2-3 tbsp. crème fraîche
1 tbsp. brown sugar
2 tbsp. unsweetened cocoa powder
1 tbsp. sesame seeds with 1 tsp. brown sugar
1 sourdough galette dough

Making the dough:

In a food processor, pulse flour, salt, and cold butter (cubed) until it crumbles.

Add the chilled sourdough starter and the iced water and pulse until the mix comes together. It does so in no time, and it's important not to overwork the dough.

Pour the mix onto a pastry board and work the dough until it all comes together. Form a disk and cover in plastic wrap.

Chill the dough in the fridge for at least an hour; you can make this dough in advance and chill overnight before using it. You can freeze the dough for up to 3 months. If you do freeze it, thaw it in the fridge overnight before use.

Making the filling:

Pre-heat oven to 400°F.

Caramelize the sesame seeds in a small non-stick skillet with the ½ tbsp. of brown sugar. Do this with low heat and constantly moving the seeds around, as they tend to burn easily. When they are caramelized, approximately 10 minutes, transfer to a small bowl to cool down and set aside. Finely slice the pears.

On a lightly floured surface, start rolling out the dough forming a disk. When it begins to thin out, sprinkle the seeds all over the crust (make sure the seeds have cooled down, as we always want to work with cold pastry), then cover with plastic wrap and roll out the dough until you form a 20-inch disk. Half-way through the rolling process, move the crust to a silicone mat that you will place onto the round baking dish; this will make the transfer much easier when the crust starts to be thin (if you notice the crust becoming too warm and difficult to manage, put it in the fridge for a few minutes and then continue).

In a small bowl, mix the cocoa powder, the crème fraîche, and the sugar. During this step, if you want, you can add a few drops of vanilla paste (or extract) or orange zest (you can add more sugar if you like sweeter desserts, just taste the cream, and follow your instinct).

Puncture the crust with a fork, then spread the crème fraîche all over the crust leaving a little less than an inch from the edges. Now layer the thinly sliced pears, then fold the edges and pinch them to seal the filling. Remember that galettes are very forgiving, so when you fold the edges, if you notice some portions have a thicker crust, use part of it to patch any small hole you might have in other areas.

Beat the egg in a small bowl and brush the entirety of the crust with an egg wash. Brush inside the small creases as well, as this will help seal any possible little hole you may have. Sprinkle the crust and the top with some brown sugar.

Bake at 400°F for 35-40 minutes until the crust is beautifully golden.

Allow to cool down for 5-10 minutes and enjoy.

CHOCOLATE AND AMARETTO "SALAMI"

FOR 8–10 PEOPLE

This beautiful and decadent dessert is another traditional one from my childhood. It is very easy to make, and it is the ultimate crowd-pleaser. Don't get confused by the name; it will look like a salami, but it tastes like pure chocolate bliss. The traditional version calls for basic dry biscotti, but I love amaretti and love their combination with dark chocolate. The secret for the perfect one is the quality of the very few ingredients: So, choose a quality dark chocolate, good amaretti, and the freshest unsalted butter.

I am using rum extract, but if you do drink alcohol, feel free to use real rum. This dessert keeps in the freezer for up to a month. I used to work in a pizzeria when I was younger, and I remember taking it out of the freezer when someone ordered it, we would only allow a few minutes for it to come down to room temperature. You can add some orange zest, and serve it with some unsweetened whipped cream.

Preparation: 20 minutes
Passive time: 2-3 hours in the fridge

250 gr. (8.8 oz.) of high-quality dark chocolate (*I like to mix 80% and 75%.*)
1 stick unsalted butter
110-120 gr. (3.8 or 4.2 oz.) sugar
2.4 tsp. (10 ml.) rum or 1 tsp. rum extract (or to taste)
1 tsp. vanilla paste or extract
2 tbsp. (15 gr.) unsweetened raw cocoa
200 gr. (7 oz.) amaretti cookies
Powdered sugar for dusting

All ingredients must be at room temperature.

Melt the chocolate in bain-marie (a double boiler works great for this). We don't need to temper the chocolate, but I like to avoid the microwave.
Once melted, allow the chocolate to cool down, and move on to breaking the amaretti in a mixing bowl.

In another mixing bowl, and with a hand mixer, cream butter and sugar (butter must be soft, at room temperature).

Add the rum, or the rum extract to the cream of butter, then add the melted chocolate and the cocoa powder.

Add the crumbled amaretti to the chocolate and mix until it becomes a smooth batter.
Transfer the batter to a big sheet of parchment paper and shape it like a long salami, never

touching the mix, but allowing the parchment paper to do the work. Close the ends tightly like a candy wrap and place in the fridge for at least 2-3 hours.

Once the salami has completely hardened, it's ready to be served. Take it out of the fridge 15-20 minutes before cutting it, dust with powdered sugar (this will resemble the white mold on a salami), and serve sliced like a salami. You can add some unsweetened whipped cream or enjoy it as is.

ACKNOWLEDGMENTS

This book wouldn't have been possible without my grandmother and my mother. They showed me the beauty and the power of simple and unpretentious cooking; they loved me unconditionally; they shared with me their secrets at the stove and their culinary wisdom.

Mom, thank you for waiting for me in the kitchen until I was ready.

This book would not have been possible without my husband, Benmont. He is my biggest fan, he believes in me when I don't believe in myself, and he loves me like I never thought I could be loved.

This book would have never been possible without Naomi Rosenblatt of Heliotrope Books. Naomi believed in this project with all her heart; she trusted me; she is the publisher of this book, the editor of this book, and the guardian angel of my words and my stories. Thank you for the trust you put in me and in my story, Naomi; I will be forever grateful.

Thank you to the amazing Instagram community that followed me from the very first show of Instagram to Table, when I made a simple Italian bruschetta. Thank you for tuning in, week after week, and for the safe dialogue, for the inspiration, for showing me your vulnerabilities and for opening your life for us all to see. I love you guys; this book is for each one of you.

Thank you, Erica Canales, for being my partner in crime during the photoshoot. Thank you for your guidance and expertise, for the makeup, and for your friendship. You are one of a kind and I am grateful to call you a friend.

A heartfelt thank you to my New York City editors and recipe editors: chefs Haskell Wells and Judy Rosenblatt. This book is better and more precise because of their attentive and meticulous work, and because of their expertise.

APPENDIX A

FOOD SUBSTITUTIONS

SUGAR If you can't find palm or coconut sugar, which I often use because less sweet than cane sugar, use a smaller quantity of brown sugar or arrope (grape reduction). Myra Bullington from Pennsylvania asked, via Instagram, how to substitute vincotto, arrope, since it's hard to find in the United States. Try sweet soy sauce (largely available in Indonesian, and Asian food stores). This is a great substitute when cooking savory dishes or bitter greens, to marinate tofu and tempeh, or to add to a curry. In sweet preparations, I would recommend a bitter caramel, British golden syrup, or a very small amount of molasses.

BUTTER Any butter can be substituted with vegan butter. For baking and making pies, to answer Mary Beth Powell's question from Instagram, I love cashew or almond butter (my favorite is Kite Hill). I also use them to sauté vegetables and to make vegan béchamel sauce. However, I am still looking for the perfect one to make buttercream.

MILK When substituting milk for non-dairy, use unsweetened oat milk rather than almond. Since I have gone 99% vegan, I make everything with oat milk, from béchamel to pastry cream. Soy or rice milk are also great substitutes for cooking. When baking, however, my favorite is always almond, always unsweetened, either plain or vanilla.

PASTA Laura Schwartz from Pennsylvania (via Instagram) asked a question about pasta. When to use which one? This topic could be the subject of an entire book, but I'll share with you some of my favorite combinations: Whenever I make tomato-based sauce, I want a pasta the thick sauce can hold on to, like rigatoni, penne rigate, pipe rigate, that are ridged (rigate). When it comes to creamy sauces, I love fusilli or bowties. For *aglio, olio and peperoncino* (garlic, olive oil and chili flakes) I love a classic spaghetti, as well as for a *cacio and pepe*. Tagliatelle and pappardelle, any egg pasta, is great when you want a richer dish, and it works well with either tomato-based, cream-based, or vegetable-based sauce. Pasta is fun to play with, and there isn't really a strict right or wrong. Have fun with shapes and cuts you have not tried before and get creative in matching them with your desired condiments. In Italy, the choice of pasta is also regional, so there are types that go with pretty much any condiment and sauce, because they are very versatile. Penne, fusilli, and ziti, for example, get chosen over others for mostly cultural and traditional reasons.

DOUGH   For the galette dough, if you don't have sourdough starter, use the same amount of flour as this recipe: a few drops of apple cider vinegar, and a tbsp. of iced water (or as much as needed) until the dough comes together into small crumbs, just as it would for a pie. When I make pumpkin pie, I use the recipe for dough that you find in this book on page 238, adding 2 tbsp. of brown sugar and 1 tsp. of ground ginger.

ALCOHOL   Tracy Gromek Seaman (via Instagram) is sensitive to alcohol and can't have it. So, she asked for substitutions. As a sober person, I rarely use alcohol in my dishes other than wine to deglaze; when doing so, in fact, I make sure the alcohol evaporates completely. When baking, however, I use an Italian rum extract (you can find several American brands on the market of course). This extract is what I use in my trifle on page 232 and in some cakes as well. It's alcohol-free, and it gives the dessert that touch of liquor that, I believe, sometimes can make the recipe. Alternatively, a pinch of lemon can do the trick.

HERBS   Catherine Malinin Dunn (via Instagram) asked about herbs substitution, and all I can say is that most common aromatics can easily be substituted, unless the recipe is strictly based on a specific one, like pesto Genovese, made of basil. I often use a mix of herbs, so when I don't have one, I don't necessarily miss it much. Thyme can be substituted with a smaller quantity of oregano, chives with green onions, parsley, quite often in my experience, with dill. Oh, dill is one of those herbs I do love dry as well.

PUNTARELLE   If you can't find *puntarelle*, use green Italian chicory, dandelion greens, as the perfect substitute. And per Grandma's tip: blanch it in unsalted water to get rid of some of the bitterness. When you drain the greens, drink the water. It's very good for you, and it is quite tasty.

BUDDHA'S HAND   Anna Maurya of Ohio (via Instagram) asked about *Buddha's Hand*. The best substitution I can recommend is the peel of a non-treated and organic lemon, possibly with a thick skin. You might also use Meyer lemon, with 1.5 times the amout of regular lemon zest.

VEGETABLE OIL   If you can, choose organic and possibly sunflower or almond for baking cookies. I have recently tried a vanilla extra-virgin olive oil that works also very well. In a couple of recipes in this book, I use hazelnut oil. If you can't find it, substitute with walnut or sunflower oil. If you can, avoid canola oil. Peanut oil is great for frying.

APPENDIX B

PREPARING AND FREEZING

LEEKS cut the dark green leaves, as well as the first 2-3 layers of vegetable. Pare the greenest top leaves, exposing the yellow of the stalk. Cut lengthwise down the leek and soak for 20 minutes, if using whole. Alternately, you can chop the leaves to the desired size and rinse, soaking in cold water. In that case, the chopped leek will deposit dirt at the bottom of your basin and the leeks will be spared any grit when they are strained.

VEGETABLE SKINS AND SCRAPS Whenever you cut the ends of leeks, zucchini, carrots, and celery—or when you peel an onion or garlic—don't throw away any of it! Rather, freeze the scraps and use them to make stock (onion peels are pure gold for stock, they will enhance the flavor tremendously).

ROSEMARY I am not a fan of dry rosemary. When dried, in fact, it tends to change flavor. Try to have some fresh or frozen rosemary at hand. Often, at the end of summer, I harvest all my herbs and freeze them. They keep their original flavor this way, from basil to parsley, chives, sage, and thyme.

LAVENDAR Eileen Allen of New Jersey, (via Instagram) asked me about lavender. Which one to use? Dry, honey, syrup...my favorite is honey lavender. I love to use it when I bake, in my tea, on a piece of toast. But I know it's not easy to find—it takes a long time to make. Infusing the honey with fresh lavender flowers is a labor-intensive practice into which only a few honey producers venture, for pure passion.

I have used the syrup (that I can only buy online) for honey lavender lemonade and to make lavender caramel or to drizzle on a cake when I run out of time. It's practical and convenient, and the flavor is gentle, elegant, and mild. The trickiest of all is the use of lavender flowers, and that's because the aroma is very intense—so much so that using too much of it can really transform the most amazing cookie into an inedible bar soap. My advice on dry lavender is to start with a little, maybe using mortar and pestle. And then taste the dough. Remember that, with lavender and other strong essences like rosewater and orange blossom, we always want the hint, the suggestion that there is a floral ingredient, never a loud statement. I like to have a bite of a lavender cookie and wish for more.

APPENDIX C

ABOUT TOMATO SAUCE

If you are not making your own tomato sauce from scratch, you might want to choose a brand of each tomato product that is regularly available in your region to familiarize yourself with its acidity.

If you don't want to use sugar in your tomato sauce to offset the acidity of the tomato, add a splash of oat milk to the sauce when you start cooking it.

Medusa Wilbury (via Instagram) asked how to enhance a basic tomato sauce, how to transform it into a "new dish:" If you add some vegan cream (or dairy heavy cream) and vodka, you will have a beautiful new pasta sauce. Adding vegetables like green beans and vegan ragù will also "transform" a basic tomato sauce (I do this often).

You can spread on a bruschetta, maybe with some chili flakes and garlic, or add roasted eggplant and vegan feta or goat cheese; add it to tofu meatballs, to a minestrone. Or reduce it to a thick sauce, add mushrooms, and serve it over a warm polenta. I love working with tomato sauce so much because it is creatively very rewarding.